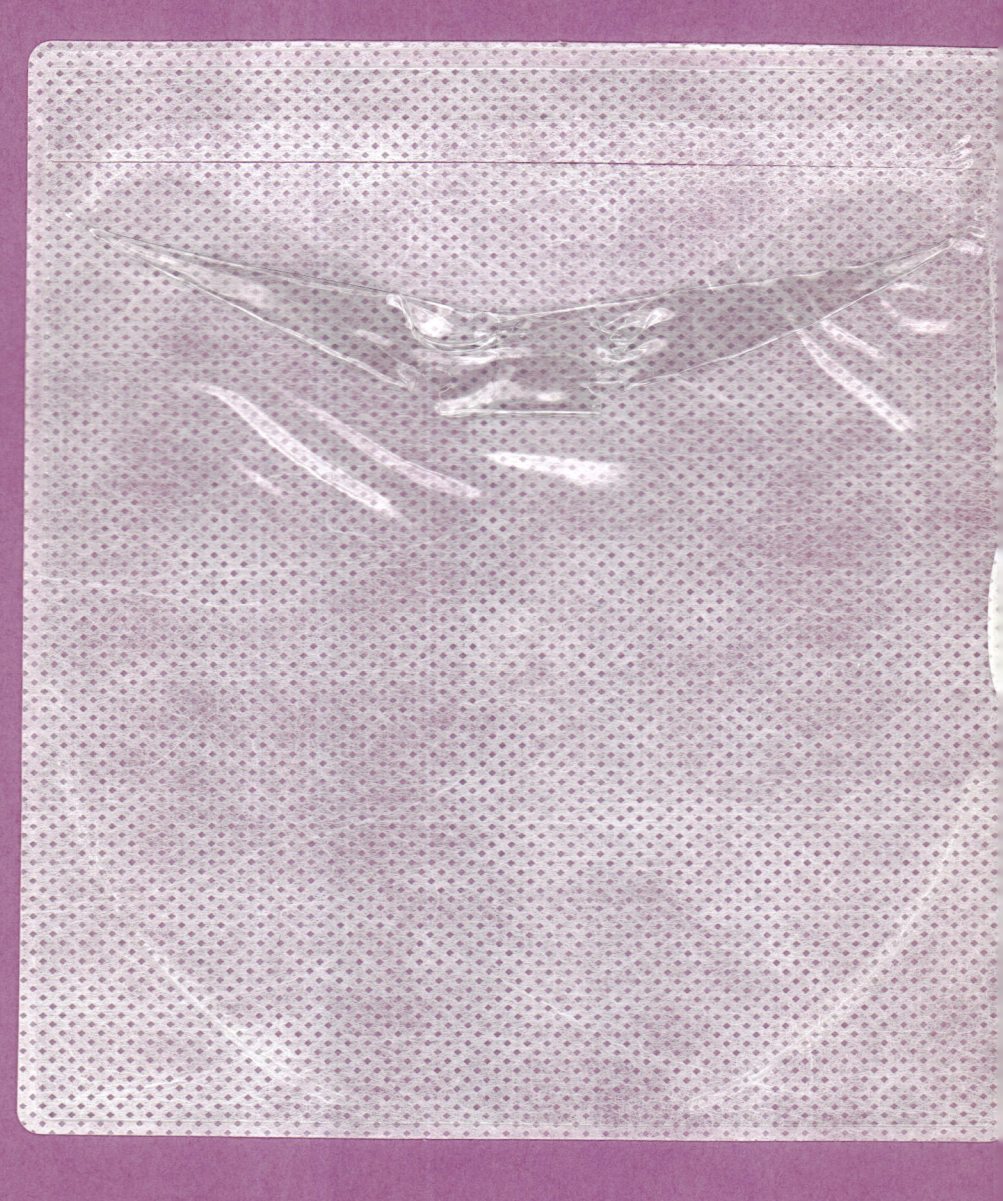

Petit Pattern Book

Petit Pattern Book
Japanese Style

Published in 2006 by BNN, Inc.
1F 35 Sankyo Bldg., 3-7-2, Irifune
Chuo-ku, Tokyo 104-0042 Japan
info@bnn.co.jp
www.bnn.co.jp

Art Direction: Masanari Nakayama (2m09cmGRAPHICS)
Book Design: Shota Yamagiwa (2m09cmGRAPHICS)
Pattern Design: MASTERPIECE INC. + Takeshi Kitaoka (Ac2)
Photo Assistant: Rie Kaneko
Translation: R.I.C. Publication Asia Co., Inc.

ISBN 978-4-86100-390-5

Printed in Japan by Shinano, Ltd.

おしゃれなパターン素材集

和・きもの柄

Petit Pattern Book

Japanese style

はじめに

「こんなパターン集がほしかった！」
いままでありそうでなかった、おしゃれな素材集の誕生です。デジタルなのに、なんだか味のあるパターンたち。紙に出力するだけで、とってもかわいいプリントになります。CD-ROMには、Illustrator用EPSファイルとPhotoshop用JPEGファイルで、本に掲載しているすべてのパターンがデータ収録されているので、気に入ったパターンをそのまま使うのはもちろん、色を変えたりサイズを変えたり、あなただけのオリジナルパターンをつくることもできます。お部屋のアクセントにしたり、デイリーの小物をリメイクしたり、大切な人へのプレゼントを包んだり。メインに、背景に、ピンポイントに、パターンを生かした手作りグッズで、日々の暮らしをいっそう楽しく演出しましょう。

Introduction

"At last - the collection of patterns I wanted!"

The collection of stylish patterns, which everyone has been waiting for, is finally available. Although they are digital images they have their own personalities. You can make pretty prints just by outputting on paper. In the CD-ROM provided, EPS files for Illustrator and JPEG files for Photoshop are to be found; because they contain the data for all the patterns in the book, you can not only use any patterns you like as they are, but you can also change colors or sizes, or make your original patterns. You can use them to match the decoration of your room, to remake objects you use everyday, or as paper to wrap presents for people who are important to you. When you make original items, use the patterns to form the main part of your design, as a background, or as a focal point. They will surely liven up your everyday life.

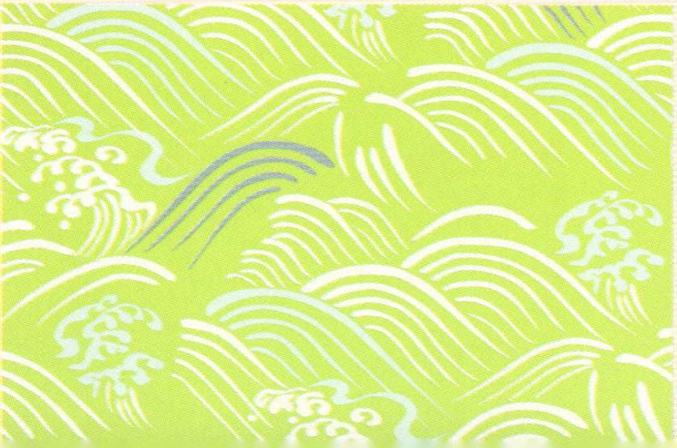

contents

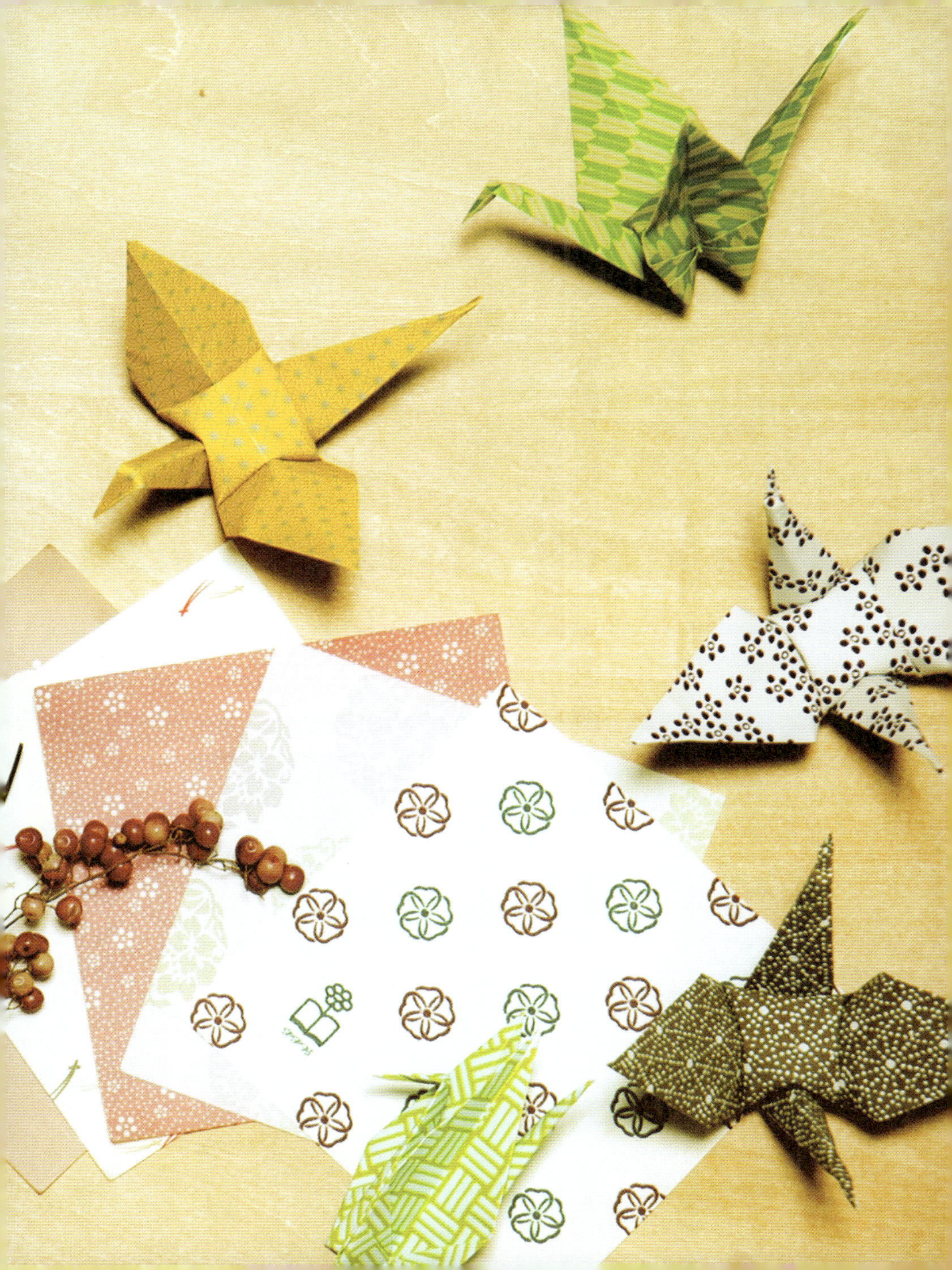

things you can make with patterns

パターンをつかったあれこれ

Petit Pattern Book
Japanese style

和・きもの柄

001〜140

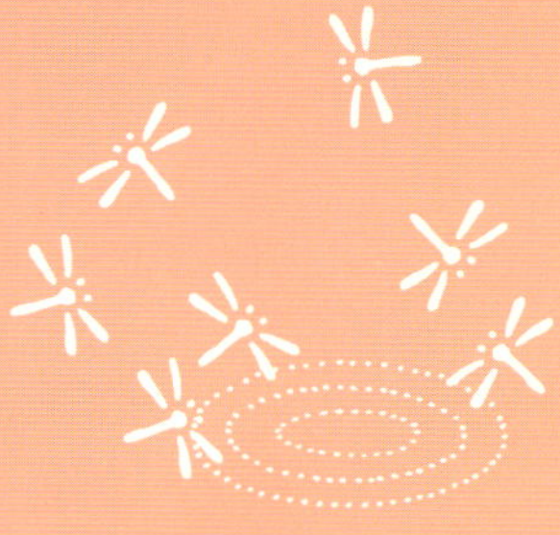

Petit Pattern Book

Japanese style

001 和・きもの柄 *Japanese style*

005
和・きもの柄 *Japanese style*

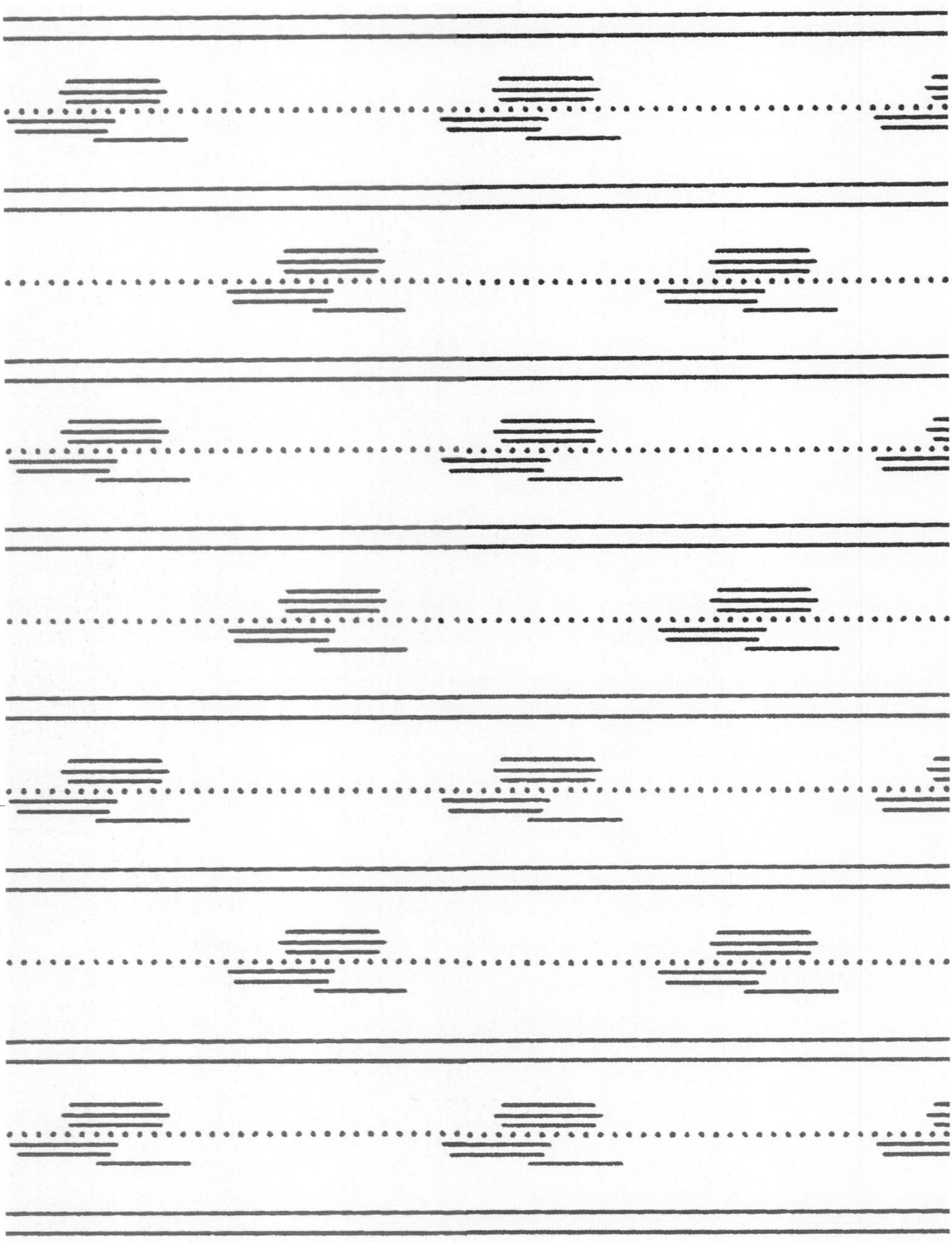

•009 | 和・きもの柄 *Japanese style*

•014 | 和・きもの柄 Japanese style

•015 | 和・きもの柄 *Japanese style*

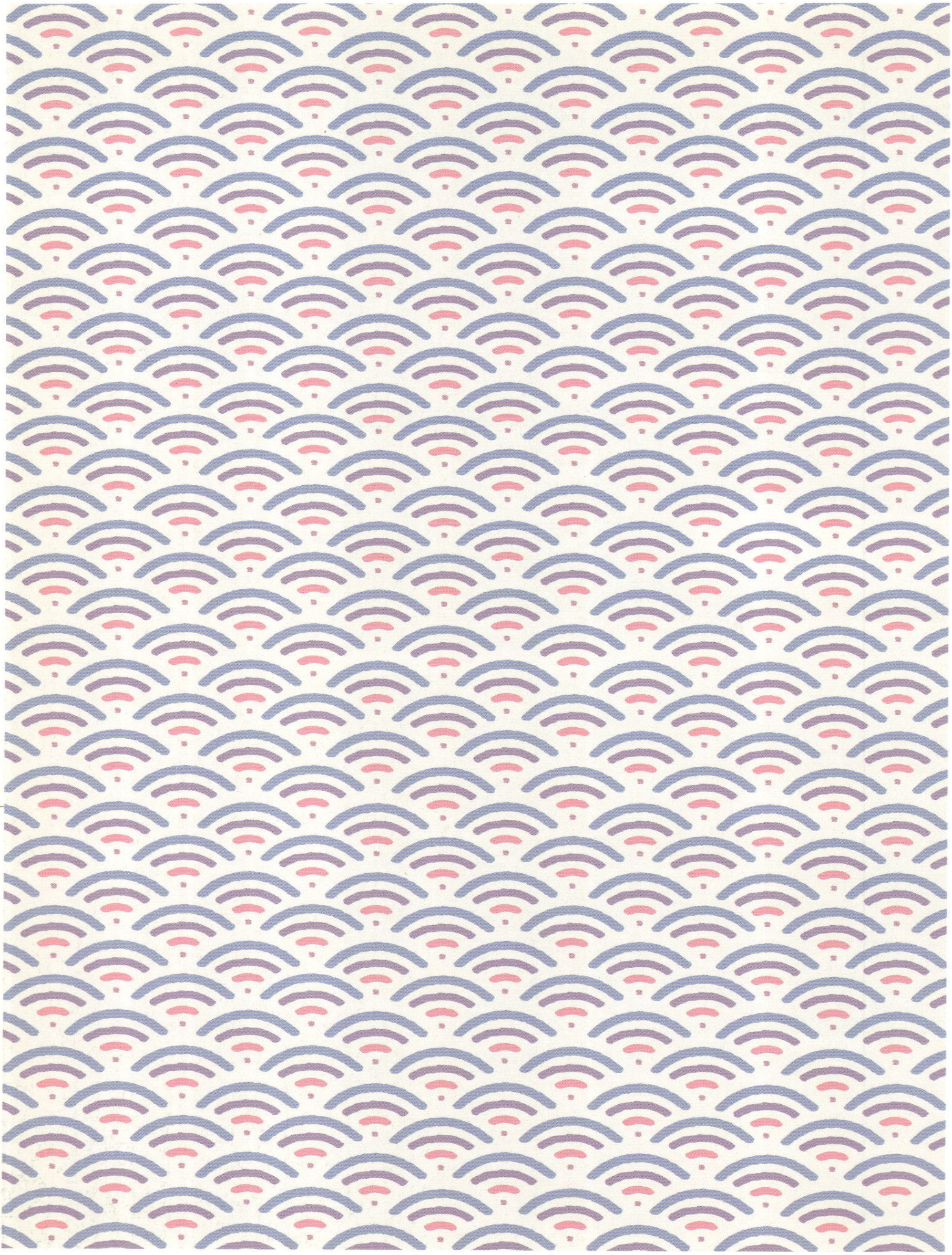

•017

和・きもの柄 *Japanese style*

018 和・きもの柄 *Japanese style*

019 | 和・きもの柄 *Japanese style*

021 和・きもの柄 Japanese style

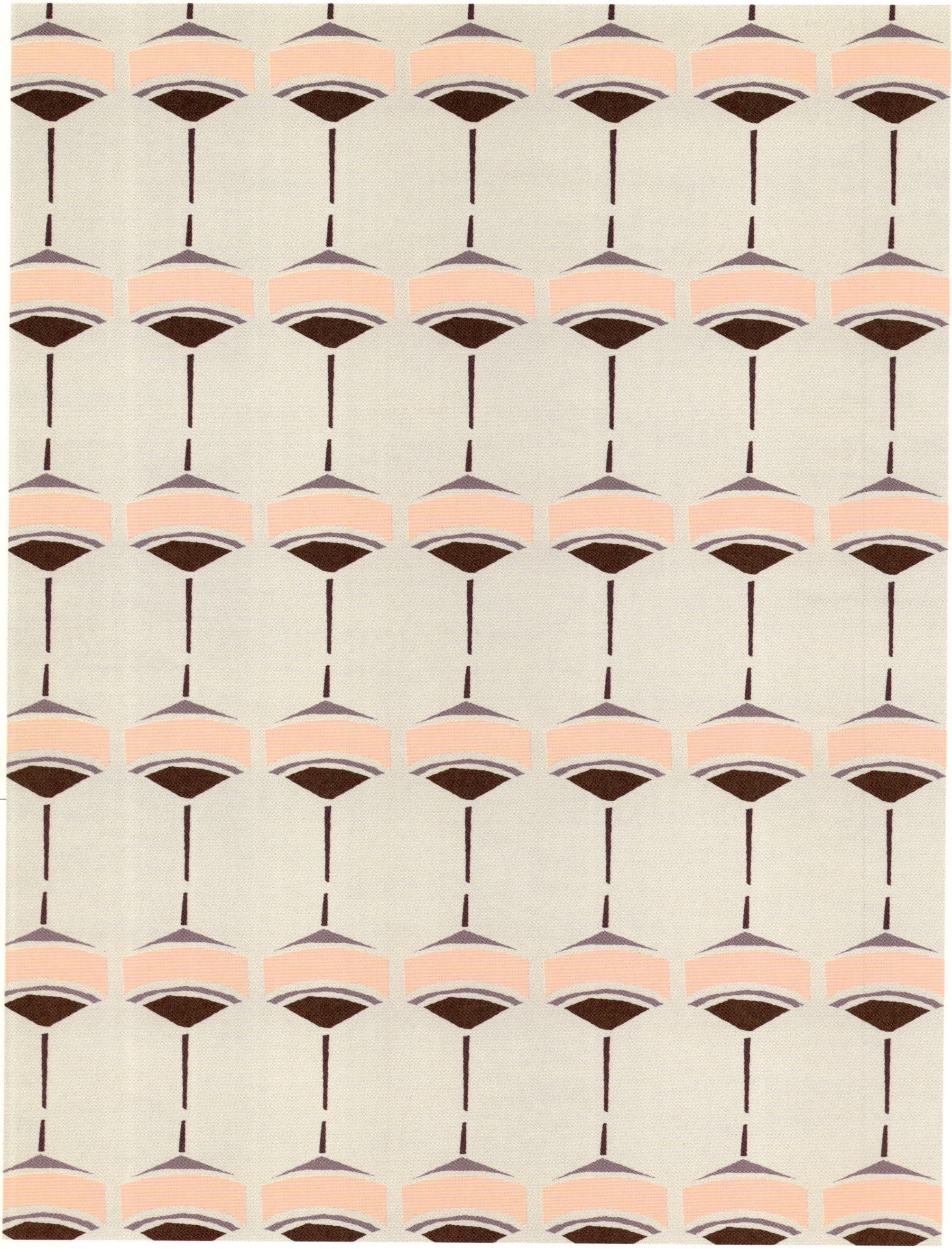

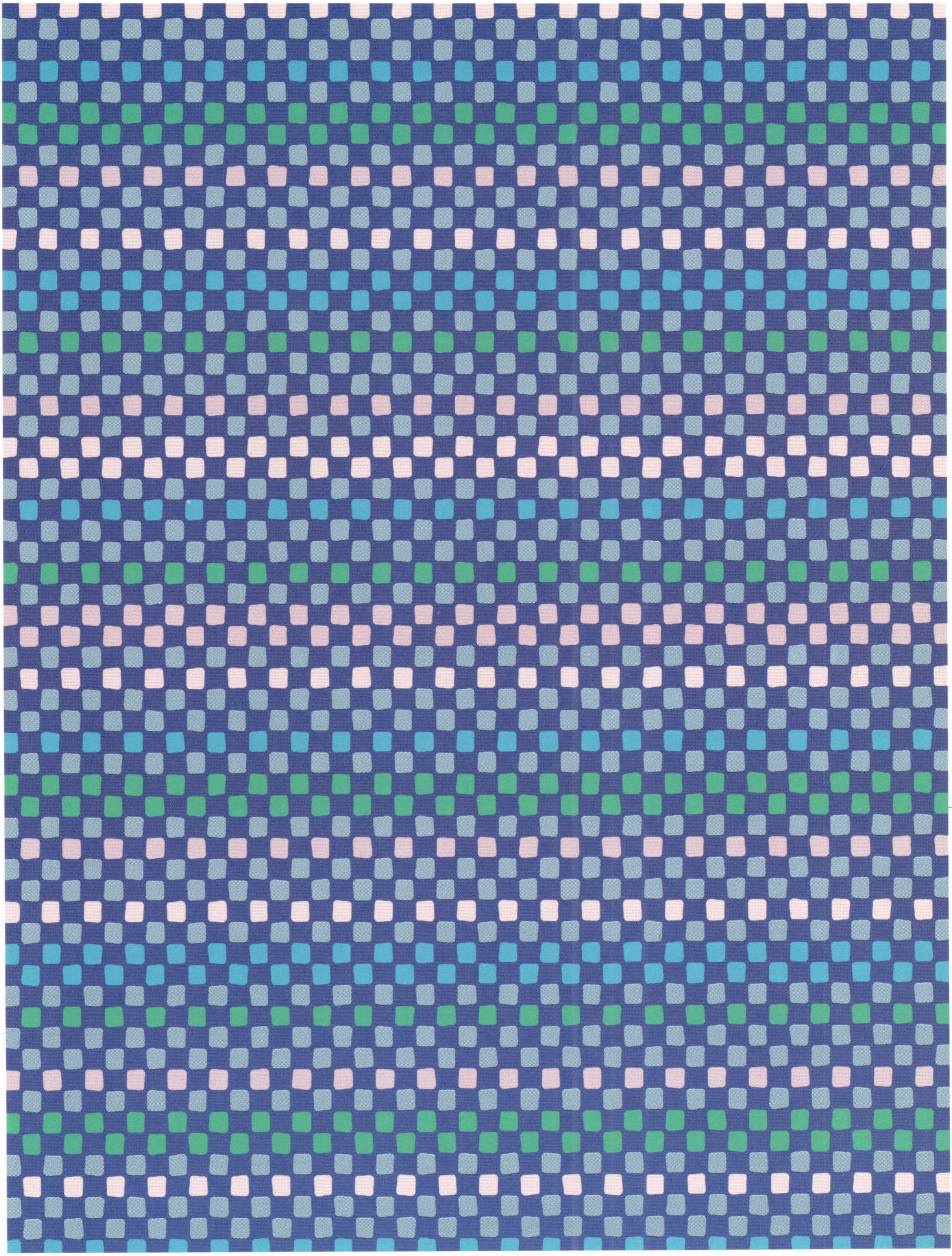

027

和・きもの柄 *Japanese style*

028

和・きもの柄 *Japanese style*

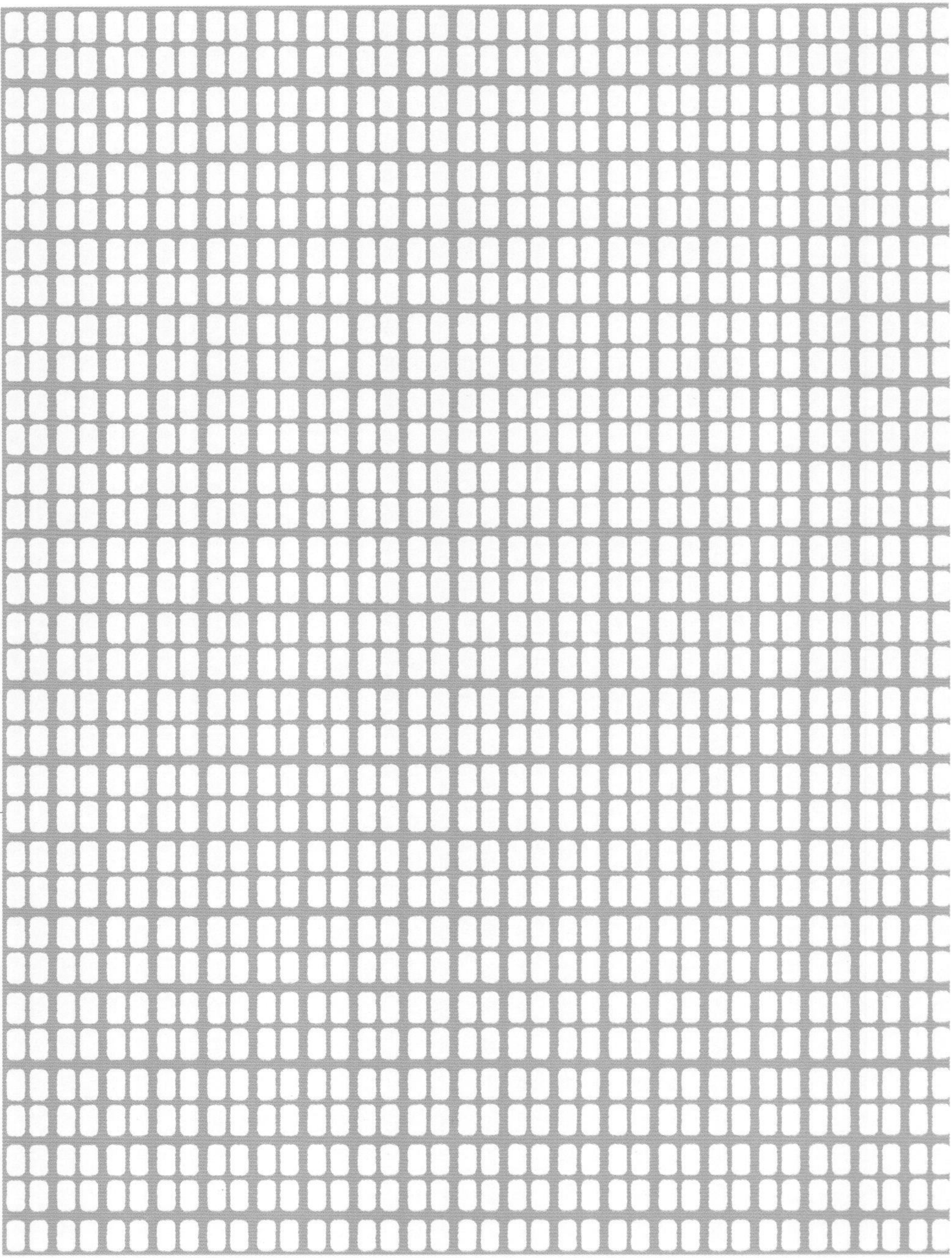

029

•030 | 和・きもの柄 *Japanese style*

032 | 和・きもの柄 *Japanese style*

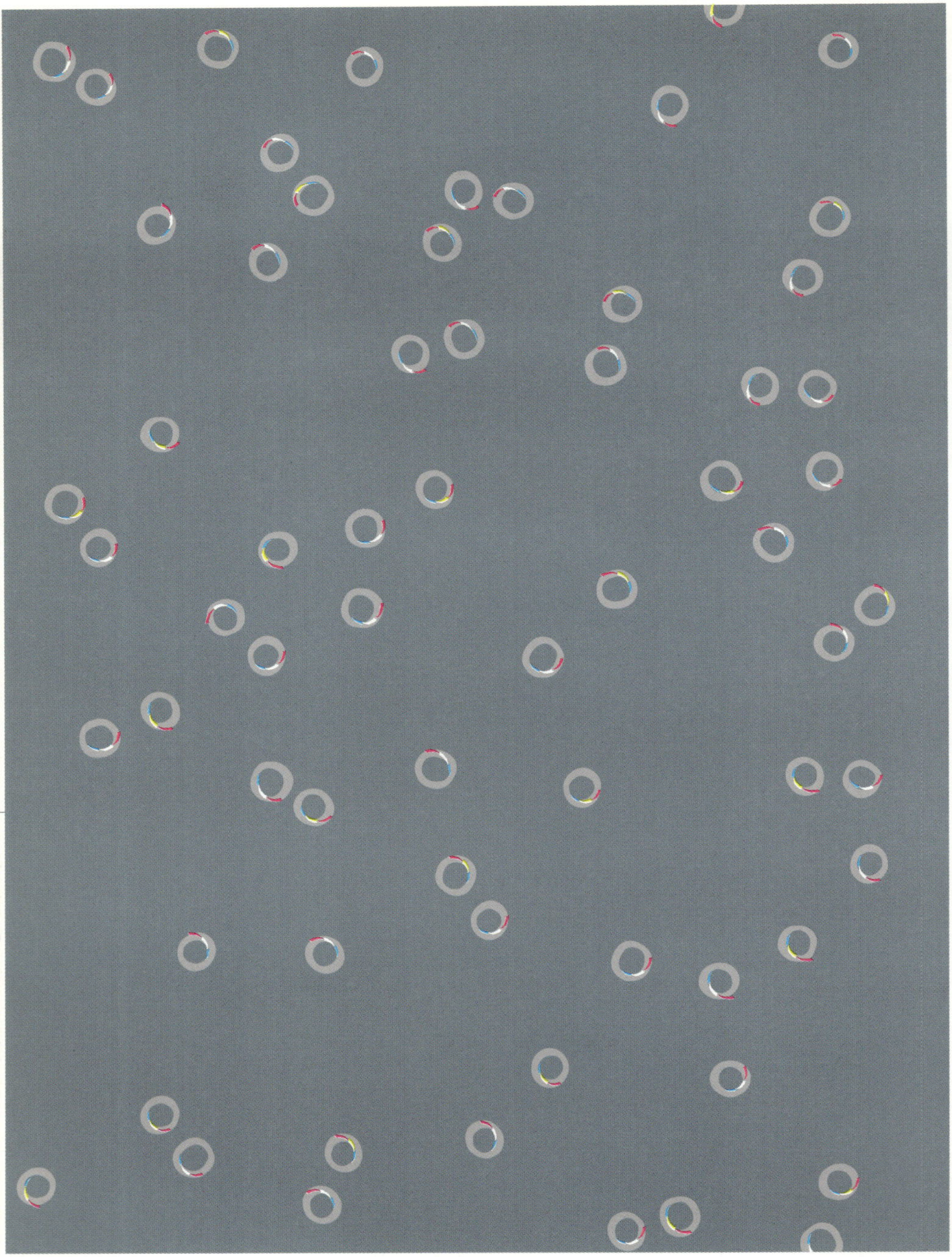

035

036

037 和・きもの柄 *Japanese style*

039

040 和・きもの柄 *Japanese style*

042

●044

●047 | 和・きもの柄 *Japanese style*

●049 | 和・きもの柄 *Japanese style*

050 和・きもの柄 Japanese style

•051 和・きもの柄 *Japanese style*

•052 和・きもの柄 *Japanese style*

053 和・きもの柄 Japanese style

056 和・きもの柄 *Japanese style*

058

060
和・きもの柄 Japanese style

061
和・きもの柄 *Japanese style*

●062 和・きもの柄 *Japanese style*

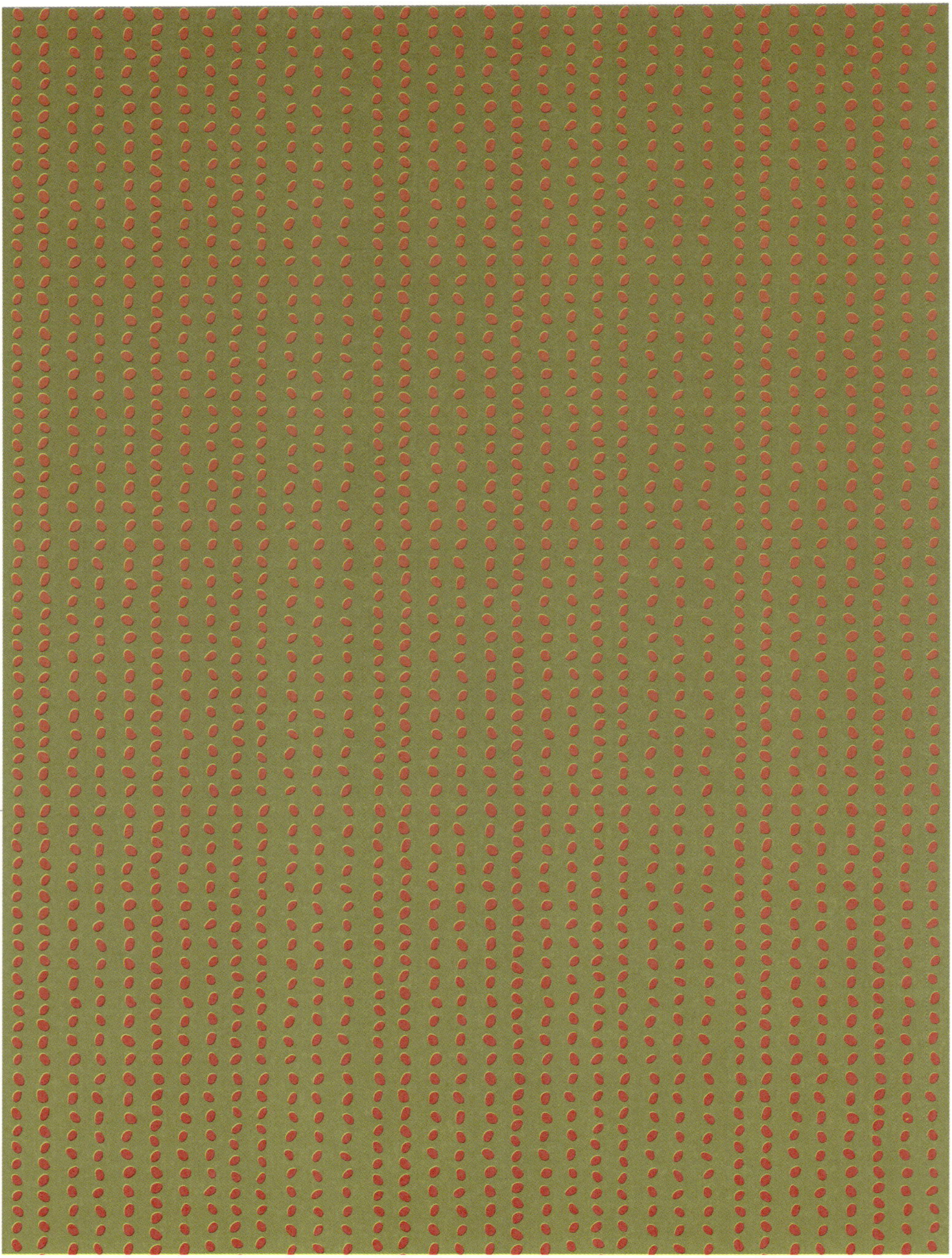

•063

和・きもの柄 *Japanese style*

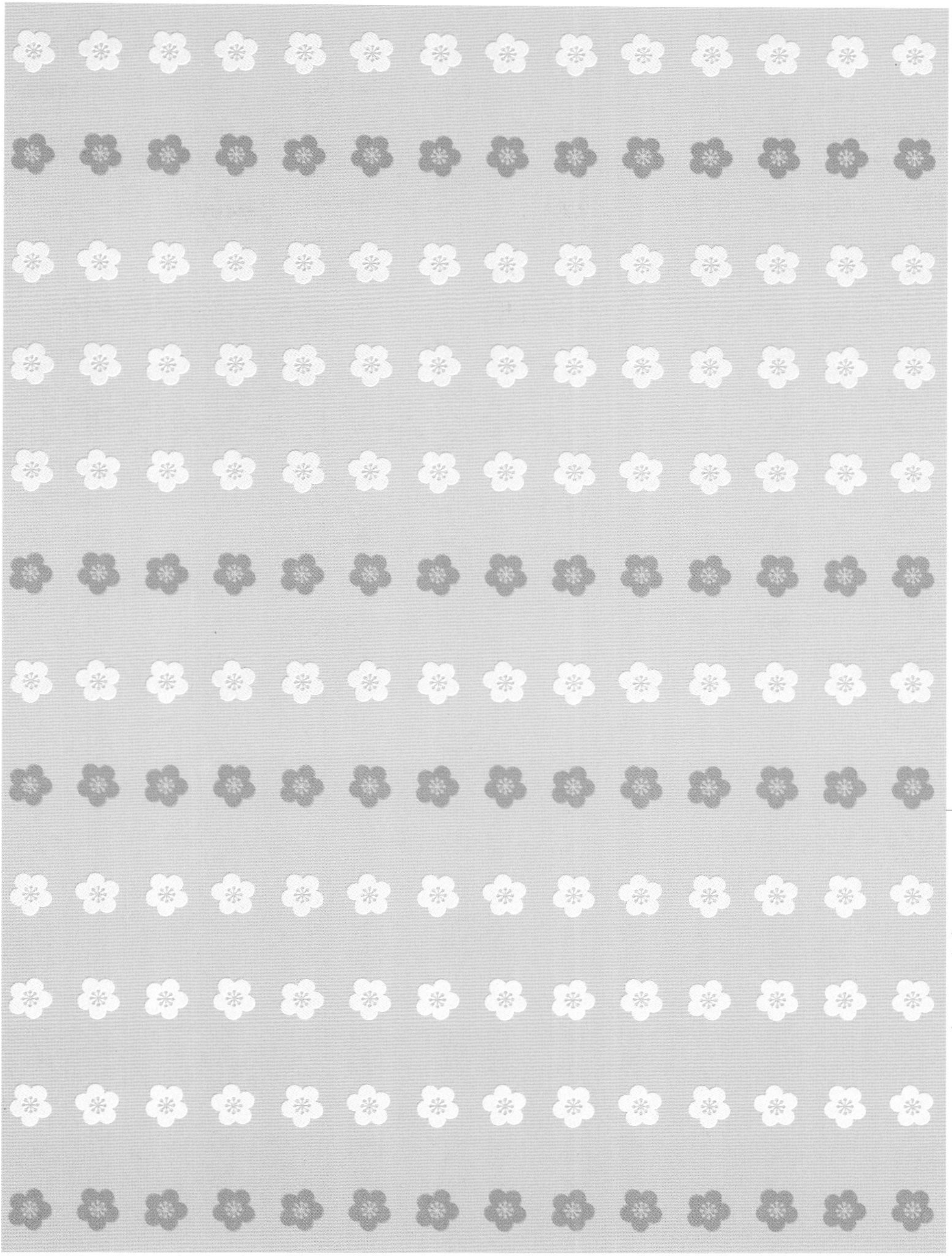

•064 和・きもの柄 *Japanese style*

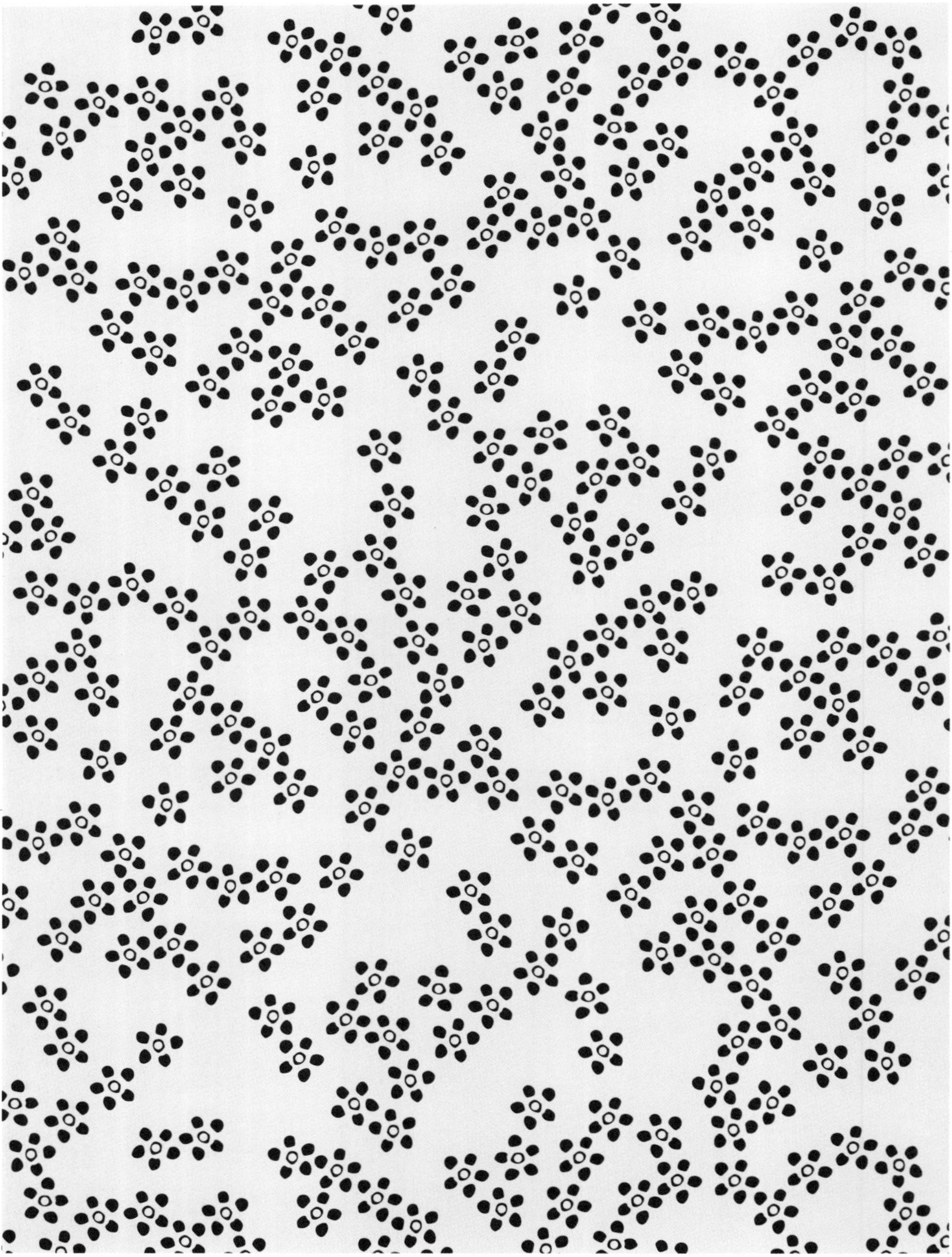

065 和・きもの柄 *Japanese style*

•067 和・きもの柄 *Japanese style*

068 和・きもの柄 *Japanese style*

●071

和・きもの柄 *Japanese style*

●073

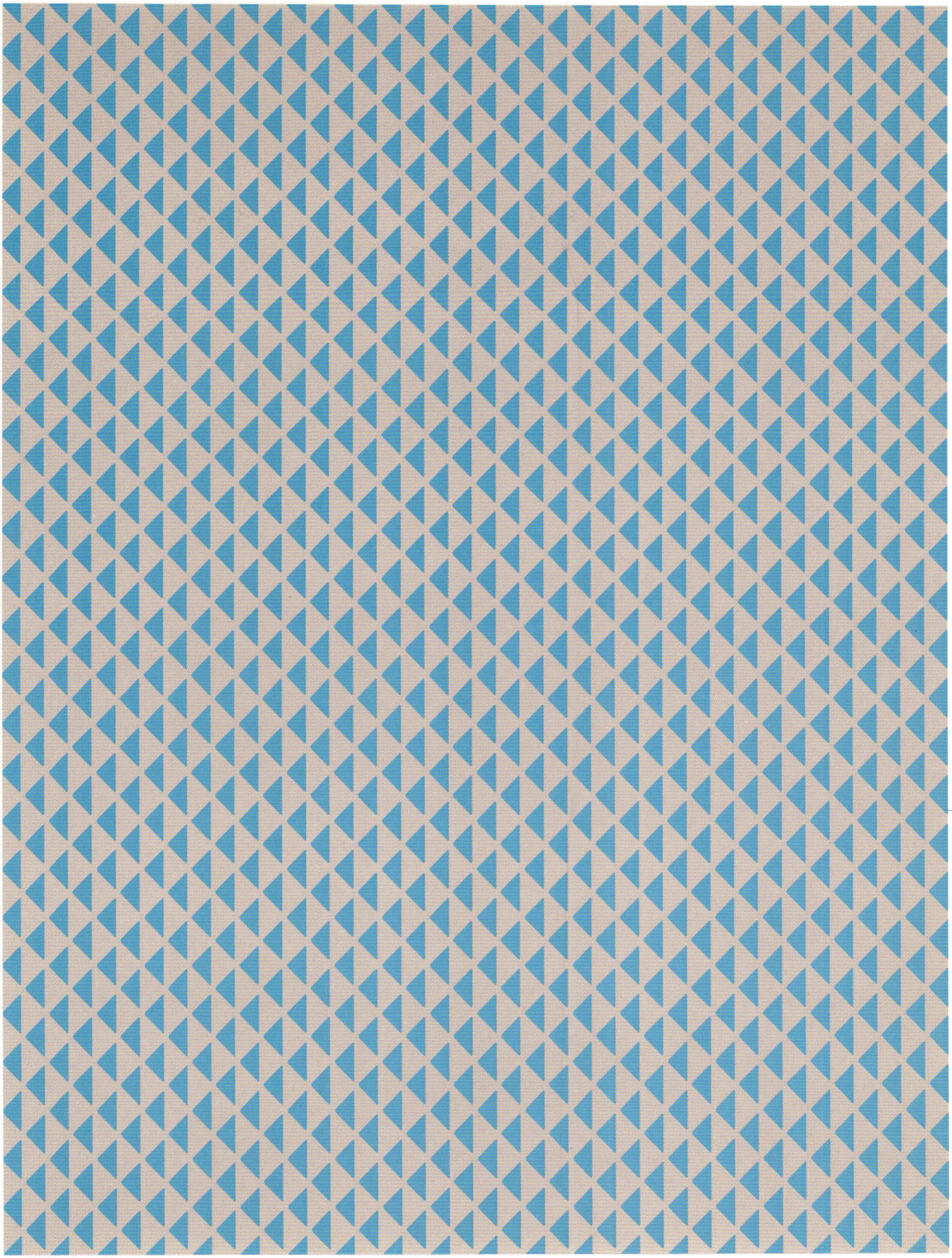

076
和・きもの柄 *Japanese style*

•078 和・きもの柄 *Japanese style*

•079

080

和・きもの柄 *Japanese style*

081 和・きもの柄 *Japanese style*

084 和・きもの柄 *Japanese style*

•085

086
和・きもの柄 Japanese style

090 和・きもの柄 *Japanese style*

091

•095 和・きもの柄 *Japanese style*

097

098 和・きもの柄 Japanese style

099

101
和・きもの柄 Japanese style

• 102

103

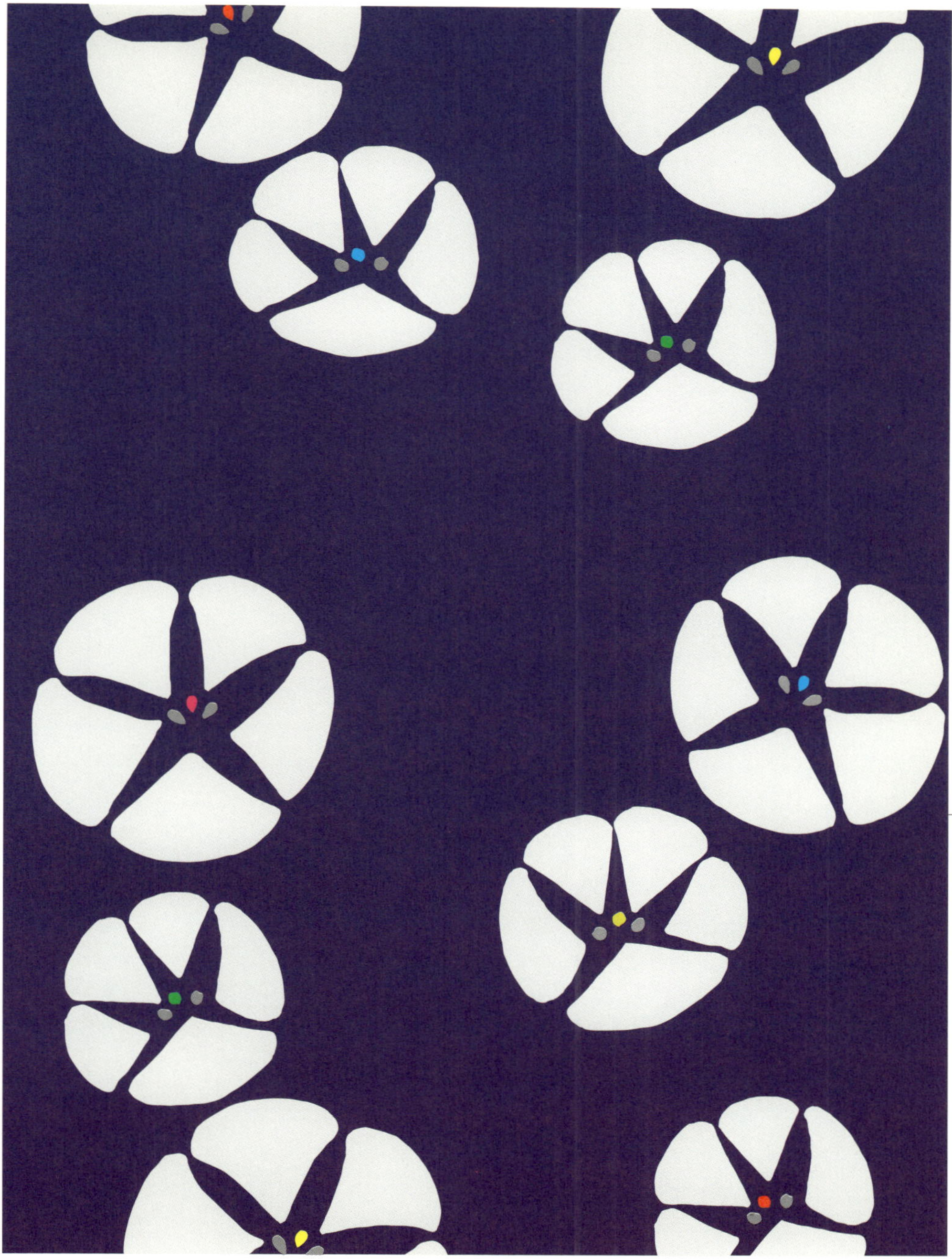

105 和・きもの柄 *Japanese style*

109 和・きもの柄 *Japanese style*

111 和・きもの柄 *Japanese style*

121 和・きもの柄 *Japanese style*

•122 | 和・きもの柄 *Japanese style*

123 和・きもの柄 *Japanese style*

•124 和・きもの柄 *Japanese style*

•125 和・きもの柄 *Japanese style*

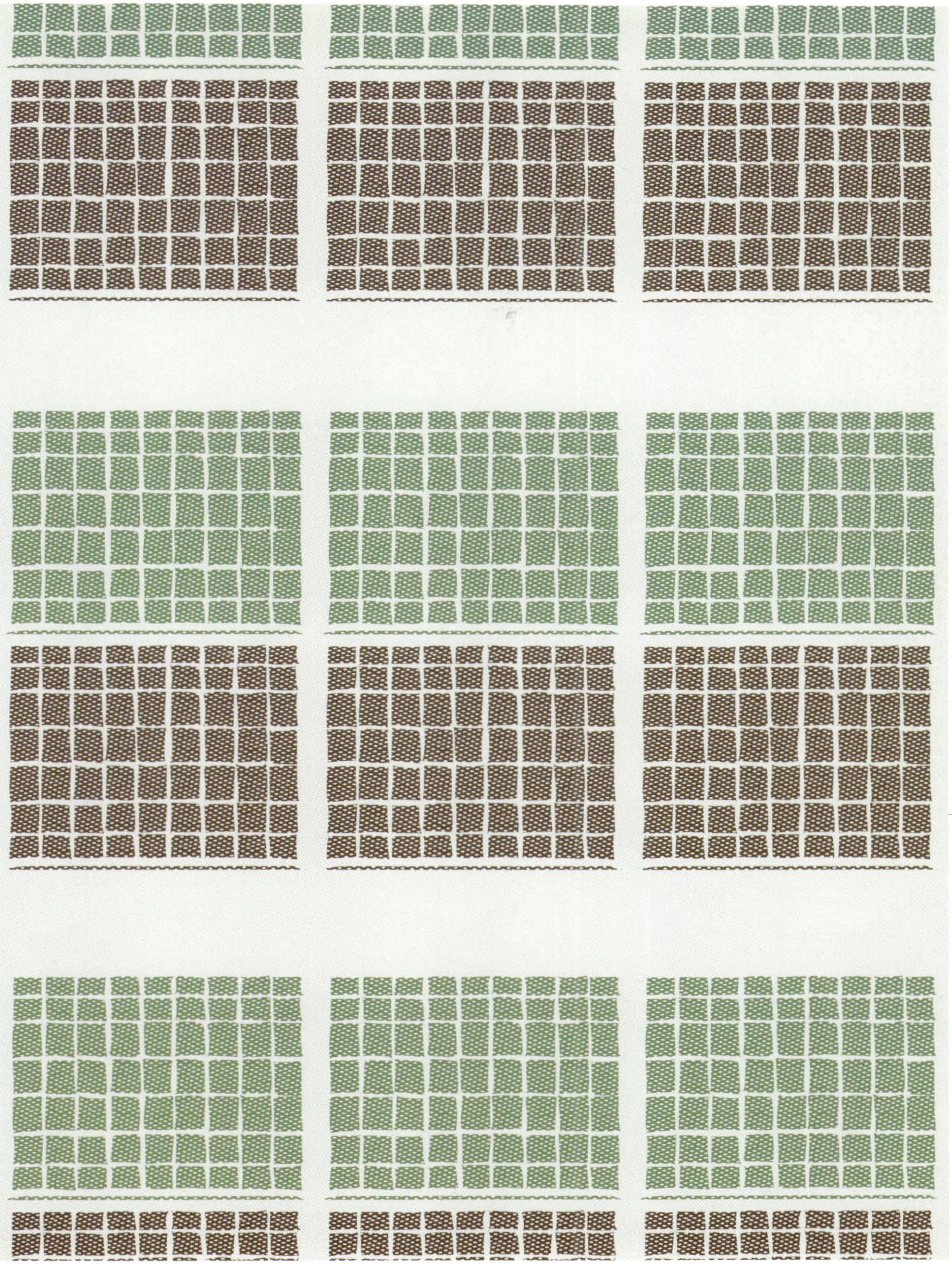

132

135 和・きもの柄 Japanese style

140

パターンの使い方

(Photoshop & Illustrator)

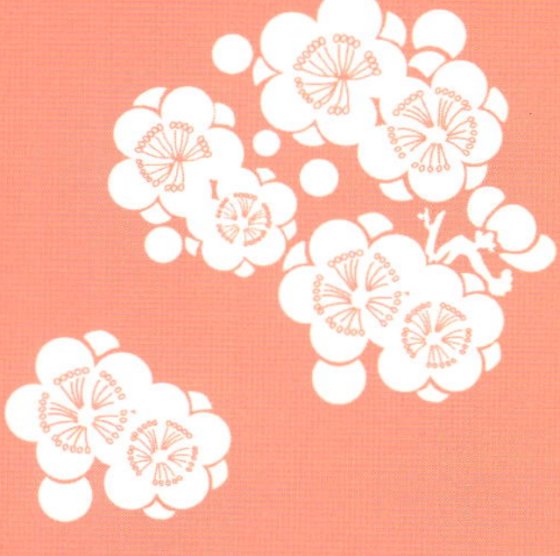

Petit Pattern Book

how to use patterns

パターンの使い方 *how to use patterns*

はじめる前に

○注意すること

- CD-ROMをご使用になる前に、必ずP.175の使用許諾をお読みください。
- 本書では、Mac OS X（10.4.5）、Adobe Photoshop CS2、Adobe Illustrator CS2を用いて解説しています。Windows XP Professional SP1でも動作確認済みですが、環境が異なる場合や、操作方法が分からないときは、OSやソフトウェアに則した、お手持ちの説明書をお読みください。
- 「パターンをつかってつくるもの」（P.164-169）では、Illustratorとプリンタを使用します。

○準備

まずはCD-ROMをセットして、「Japanese-style」フォルダを開きます。必要なデータをピックアップしてデスクトップにコピーしましょう。

「Japanese-style」フォルダを開くと、「JPEG」と「EPS」と「Template」という3つのフォルダが入っています。「Template」フォルダに入っているデータは、P.164以降で使うサンプルデータです。

Mac

Win

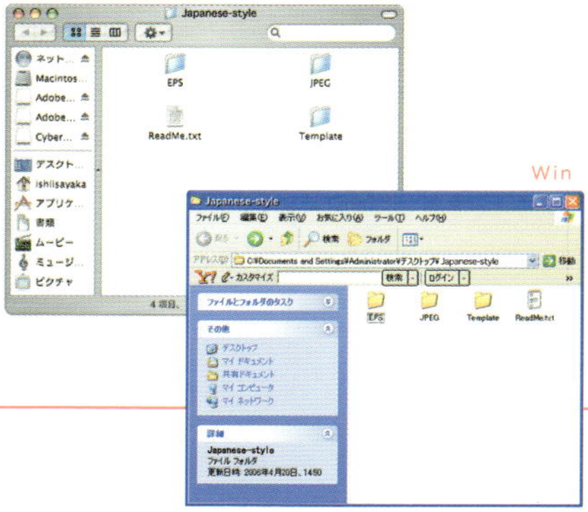

○データの種類

掲載したすべてのパターンには、それぞれJPEGとEPSの2つの形式でファイルを用意しています。
（EPSファイルは、Illustratorのバージョン8.0で保存しています）

JPEG

＊JPEGファイルとして収録したのは、350dpi（商業印刷に耐え得る解像度）に設定したときに、ほぼA5サイズの印刷面積を持つビットマップ画像。「Adobe Photoshop」をはじめとするビットマップ系のソフトウェアで編集できるほか、多くのソフトウェアで扱うことが可能です。

EPS

＊EPSファイルとして収録したのは、拡大縮小を行っても画質が劣化しない、ベクトル画像。ドロー系のソフトウェア「Adobe Illustrator」でファイルを開くと、自在にカスタマイズできます（ビットマップ系のソフトウェア「Adobe Photoshop」で開くと、「ラスタライズ」という工程を経て、ビットマップイメージに展開します）。

パターンで塗る

tiling

収録したファイルは、どれもタイリング(タイルのように敷き詰めること)が可能な、パターン(繰り返し模様)になっています。PhotoshopやIllustratorといったグラフィックソフトウェアで、パターンを登録する機能を使うと、繰り返し模様を一瞬にして好きなだけ、タイリングできます。いずれのソフトウェアでも「塗り」の設定を用いることから、本書ではこれを「パターンで塗る」と呼びます。

パターンで塗るのは初めて、という人に向けて、ここではPhotoshopとIllustratorを用いて、その設定方法を中心に説明していきます。

○データを開く

Photoshop

「ファイル」メニューから「開く」を選択し、パターンファイル(ここではJPEGファイル)を開きます。

Illustrator

「ファイル」メニューから「開く」を選択し、パターンファイル(ここではEPSファイル)を開きます。選んだパターンがページ中央に表れます。

パターンで塗る

tiling

「Photoshop」編

1. パターンを登録する

好きなパターンファイルを選んでPhotoshopで開きます。「選択範囲」メニューから「すべてを選択」を選んでパターン全体を選択し、「編集」メニューから「パターン定義」を選びます。パターンをいつでも使えるように、分かりやすい名前をつけておきます。

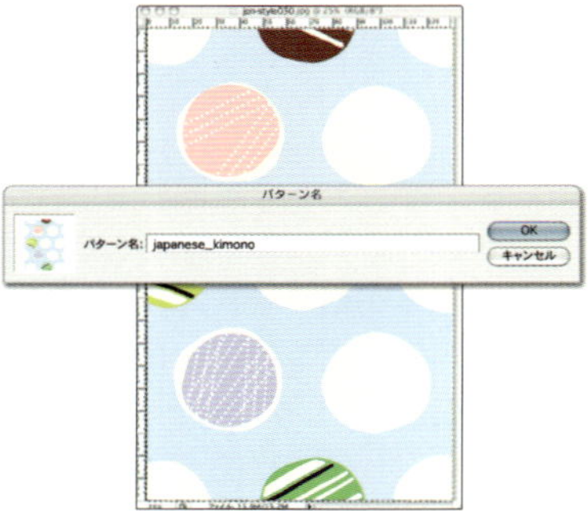

2. 登録したパターンを選ぶ

「ファイル」メニューから「新規」を選んで、パターンで塗りたい空白の画像ファイルを作成します。ツールバーの塗りつぶしツールをダブルクリックし、オプションで「パターン」を選ぶと、先ほど定義したパターンが選択できるようになります。

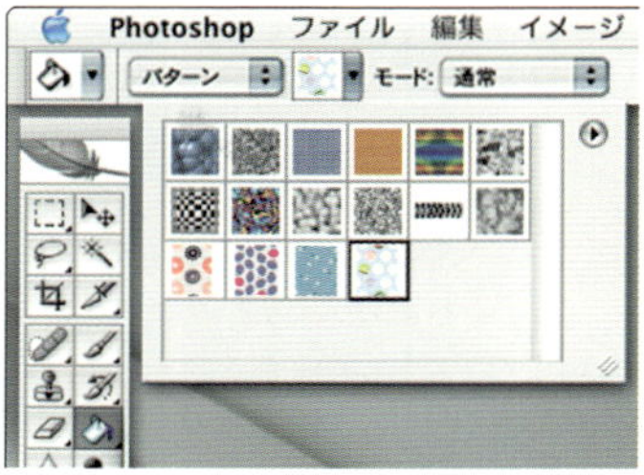

3. パターンで塗る

塗りつぶしツールで画像上の適当な箇所をクリックして、パターンで塗りつぶします。

図1

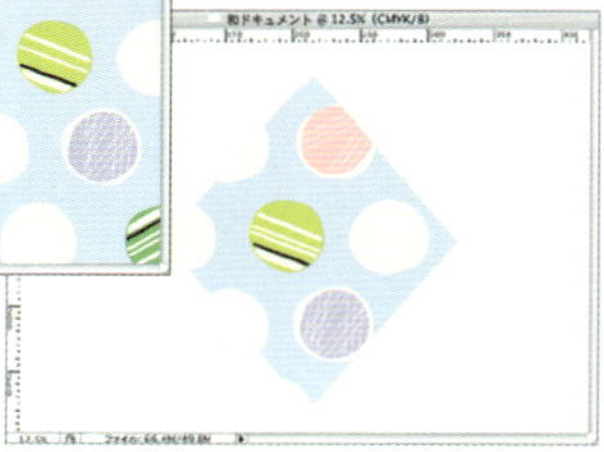

図2

＊図1は、A3サイズの空白のファイルを塗りつぶしたものです。図2のようにあらかじめ選択ツールで塗りつぶす範囲や形を選択しておくと、パターンで選択範囲内のみを塗りつぶすことができます。

パターンで塗る
tiling
「Illustrator」編

1. パターンを登録する

好きなパターンファイルを選んでIllustratorで開きます。「選択」メニューから「すべてを選択」でパターン全体を選択し、「編集」メニューから「コピー」を選ぶとパターンがコピーされます。

「ファイル」メニューから「新規」で空白のドキュメントを作成し、「編集」メニューから「ペースト」を選んでパターンをペーストします。パターン全体が選択された状態のまま、「編集」→「パターン設定」を選んで新規スウォッチを作成し、パターンをいつでも使えるように、分かりやすい名前をつけておきます。

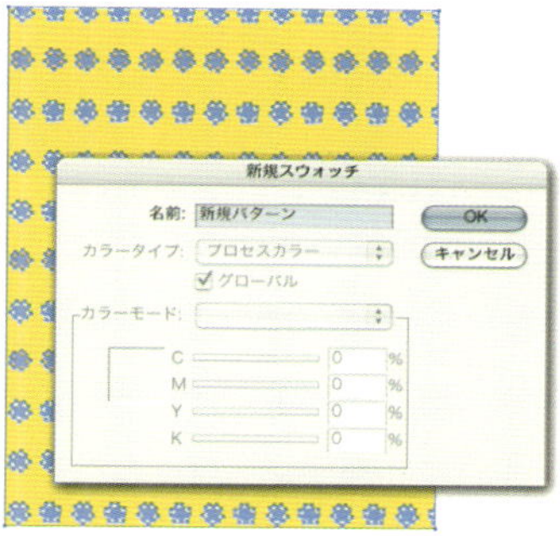

2. 登録したパターンを選ぶ

登録が終わったら、ペーストしたパターンが必要なくなるので、パターン全体が選択された状態のまま、「編集」メニューから「消去」を選んで消します。

「ウインドウ」メニューから「スウォッチ」を選び、スウォッチパレットを表示します。スウォッチパレット内に新たに作成したパターンスウォッチが登録されているので、クリックします。

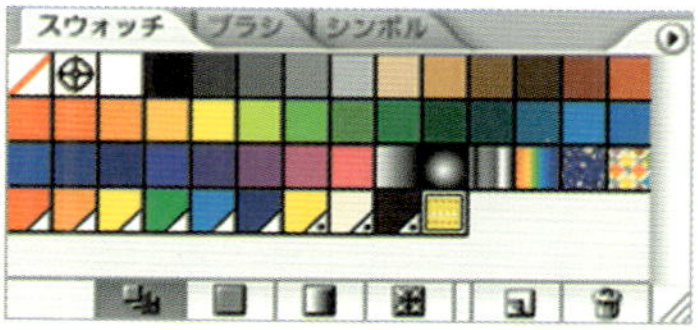

3. パターンで塗る

パターンで塗るオブジェクトを作成します。

図1

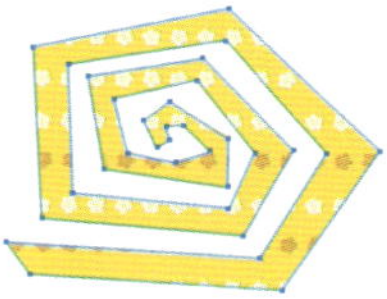
図2

＊図1は、長方形ツールで四角形を描いたものです。図2のように他のドローツールで、パターンで塗りつぶされた複雑なオブジェクトを描くこともできます。

番外編 1

「Illustrator」をつかってパターンの色を変える

Step ❶

IllustratorでEPSファイルを開き、「ウインドウ」メニューから「スウォッチ」を選択して、スウォッチパレットを表示します。続いて、変更したい色のスウォッチをダブルクリックして、「スウォッチオプション」を表示します。

＊収録されたEPSファイルのほとんどは、色や形ごとにレイヤー分けされています。それぞれのレイヤーの順番を入れ替えたり、非表示にしたり、いろいろなアレンジが可能になっています。

Step ❷

「スウォッチオプション」上にあるカラーパレットでCMYKを好きな色に変更します。その際「プレビュー」にチェックを入れておくと、色がパターンにすぐに反映されるので便利です。色が決定したら「OK」をクリックします。

＊Illustratorで開いたEPSファイルは、サイズを変えたり、形を変えたり、要素を足したり引いたりと、自由自在。でも、加工したパターンをスウォッチに登録して使いたい場合は、タイリングで繋がる部分の四辺のアートワークを、加工で崩してしまわないよう気を付けましょう。

Step ❸

1〜2を繰り返して、オリジナルパターンの出来上がり。別名で保存しておきましょう。

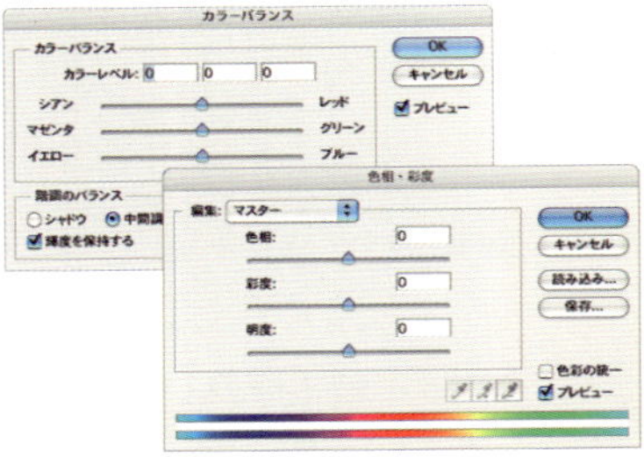

＊Photoshopで開いたJPEGファイルの色を変更することも可能ですが、複雑な輪郭で描かれたパターンは、塗りつぶしツールできれいに色を変更できないことがあります。そういった場合には、「イメージ」メニューから「色調補正」→「カラーバランス」もしくは「色相・彩度」で色味を調整することができます。同じパターンのEPSファイルをまずはIllustratorで開いて色を変更し、別名でJPEG保存したものを、次にPhotoshopで開いて使う方法もあります。

番外編 2

パターンをデスクトップの壁紙にする

Step ❶

Photoshopで壁紙に設定したいパターンのJPEGファイルを開いて、「イメージ」メニューから「画像解像度」を選択し、モニタ表示に充分な「72 dpi」に解像度を設定し直して、別名で保存します。

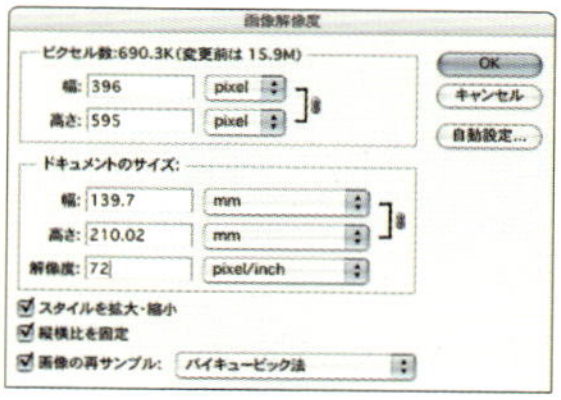

Step ❷

-for Mac-

Macでは、「アップル」メニューから「システム環境設定」→「デスクトップとスクリーンセーバ」を選択します。「フォルダを選択」から先ほど別名で保存したファイルを指定し、「タイル状に配置」にすると、デスクトップにパターンが表示されます。

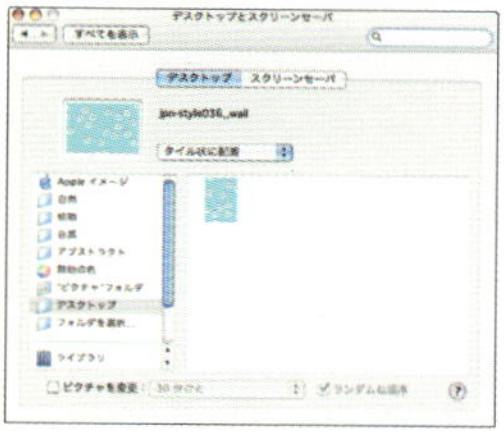

-for Win-

Windowsでは、「コントロールパネル」で「画面」を選択し、「画面のプロパティ」を開きます(デスクトップ上で右クリックして選択することもできます)。「デスクトップ」から先ほど別名で保存したファイルを指定し、「並べて表示」にすると、デスクトップにパターンが表示されます。

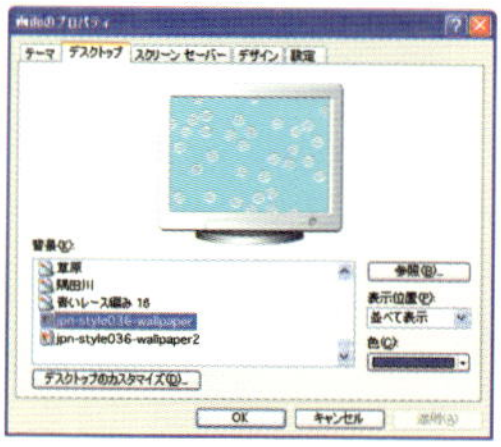

and more!

パターンをウェブサイトの背景にする

上のStep ❶で「72 dpi」に解像度を設定し直したデータは、ホームページの背景にも使えます。
この際にはJPEGファイルを、写真以外のアートワークの保存に適した、GIF形式に置き換えることをおすすめします。

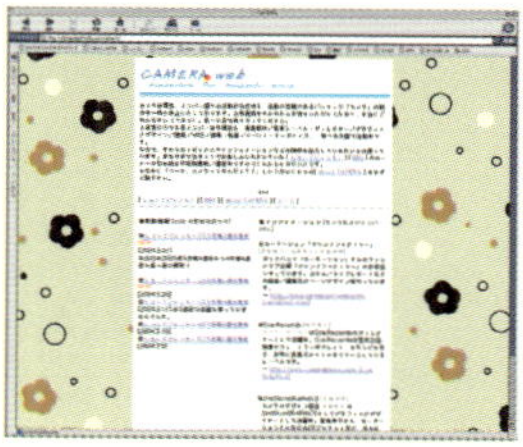

1 パターンをつかってつくるもの

ぽち袋をつくる

**お祝いやちょっとしたお礼は、手作りの
かわいいぽち袋に入れて。よろこぶ顔を思い浮かべて
パターンをセレクトすれば、気持ちがもっと伝わります。**

1

○用意するもの

印刷用紙（普通紙でも可能ですが、インクジェット用和紙などを使用すると風合いよくできます）、カッター、のり、鉄筆（なければインクの切れたボールペンや、芯を出さないシャープペンシルなどでも可）

1. 台紙データを開く

付属CD-ROMの「Template」フォルダの中にある「pochi.eps」をデスクトップにコピーし、Illustratorで開きます。

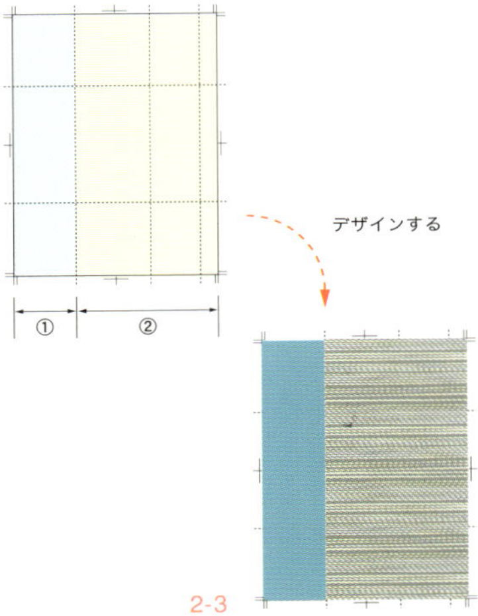

2-3

2. パターンを使ってデザインする

次に、使いたいパターンを「スウォッチ」に登録します（P.161参照）。

台紙データにはあらかじめトンボ（トリムマーク）がついています。トンボはカットや折り目をつける際に、目印となるものです。

台紙データには、①・②の2つのオブジェクトがあります。それぞれの塗りにパターンや色を設定しましょう。最終的には①・②の絵柄が折り重なって仕上がります。組み合わせを想定しながら、自由にデザインしてみましょう。

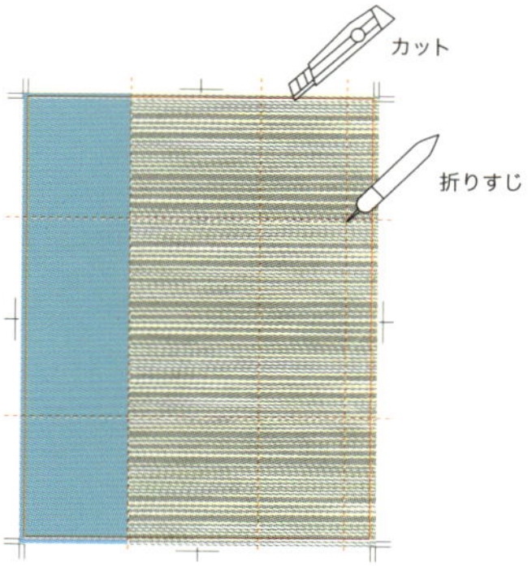

4

5

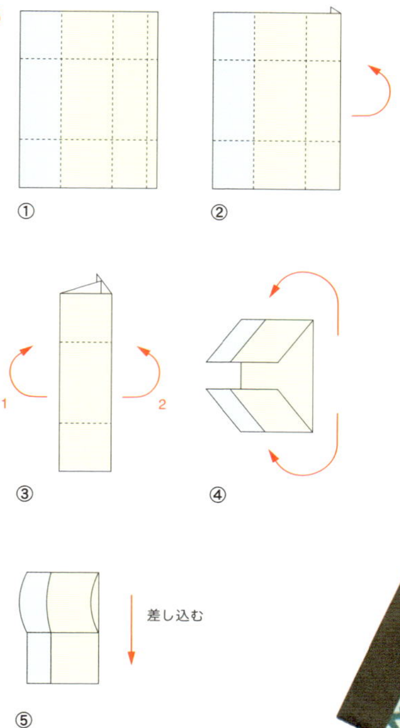

3. プリントする

デザインが完成したら、プリントします。今回はインクジェット用和紙を使用しました。

4. 折りすじを入れてカットする

プリントが終わったら、折りすじを入れてカットします。

今回CD-ROMに収録した台紙データには点線の折りトンボがついています。点線の折りトンボに定規を合わせ、鉄筆で折りすじを入れます。こうしておくとあとで折りやすくなります。

次に、コーナートンボの内側に定規をあててカットします。

5. 折りすじに沿って折っていく

カットしたら、先ほど入れた折すじに沿って、左図①～⑤の手順で折りたたんでいきます。

出来上がり!

アレンジを加えていろいろなデザインを試してみましょう。アクセントとして、飾りひもや小さく折った折り紙などをつけてもかわいいですね。

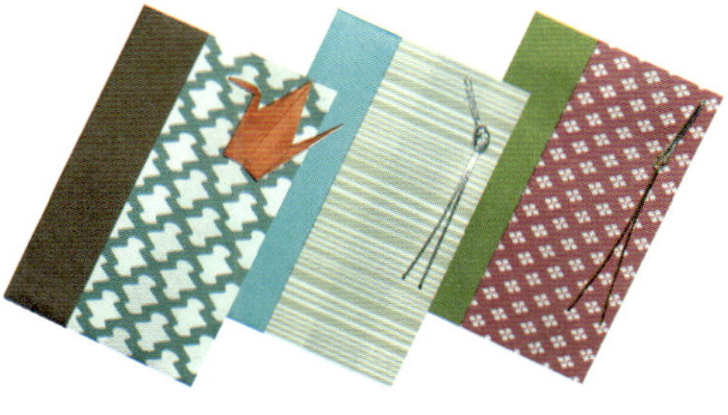

2 パターンをつかってつくるもの

匂い袋をつくる

ふんわり香り立つ和柄のサシェは、枕元に飾ったり、バッグにしのばせてみて。ぬくもりのある色を選べば、見た目にもリラックスできます。

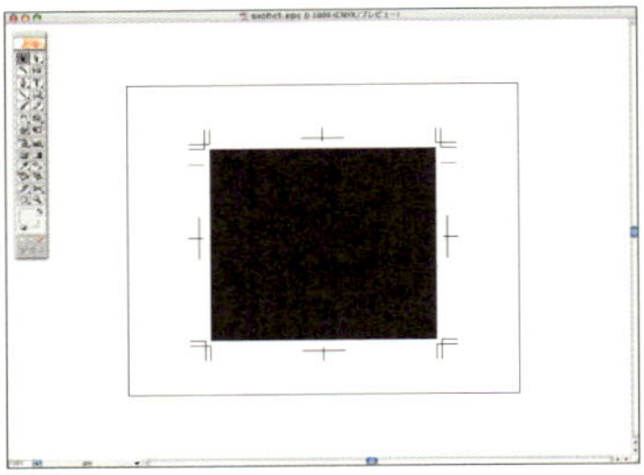

1

○用意するもの

専用布用紙、ひも、チャコペン、ミシン、手芸用ボンド、はさみ、カッターナイフ

1. 台紙データを開く

付属CD-ROMの「Template」フォルダの中にある「sachet.eps」をデスクトップにコピーし、Illustratorで開きます。

2

2. パターンで塗る

次に、使いたいパターンを「スウォッチ」に登録します(P.161参照)。選択ツールを選び、ドキュメント上のオブジェクトを選択します。選択したオブジェクトの塗りに、先ほど登録したパターンを設定します。これでデータの出来上がりです。

3

3. 専用布用紙にプリントする

プリンタに専用布用紙をセットしてプリントします。今回使用している用紙は裏面にPETフィルムが貼られたタイプのものですが、同じように用紙には表裏がありますので注意してセットしましょう(プリントの際の細かな設定は、各製品に記載されている注意事項に従って設定してください)。

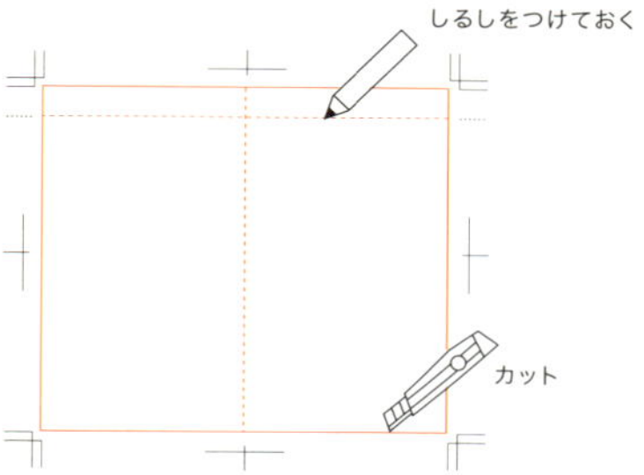

4

4. カットする

今回CD-ROMに収録した台紙データには、あらかじめトンボ（トリムマーク）がついています。トンボはカットや折り目をつける際に、目印となるものです。まずは折りトンボに沿って、チャコペンなどで折り線が分かるようにしるしをつけましょう。

次にプリントしたパターンの余白部分をカットします。カットする場合はコーナートンボの内側に定規をあてて行います。

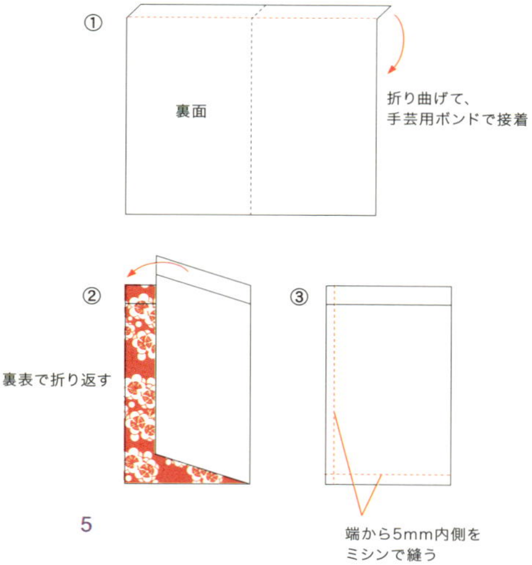

5

5. 縫製する

裏に貼られているPETフィルムをはがしてから、4でつけたしるしを目安に図の①～③のように縫っていきます。縫い合わせたら、裏返しておきます。

6

6. 中身をセットして口を結ぶ

袋が完成したら、お好みの香りを入れましょう。細かく刻んだお香を入れるのが一般的ですが、コーン型のお香やポプリなどを入れても楽しめます。最後に袋の口をひもでしばったら完成です。

出来上がり！

持ち物にさりげなくしのばせるのはもちろん、ふだんはクローゼットにかけておいてもよいですね。

3 パターンをつかってつくるもの

和綴じの手帳をつくる

スケジュールをメモしたり、日記をつけたり…。どこかやさしい雰囲気の和綴じの手帳に書きとめれば、気持ちまでゆるやかに。デスク周りも和らぎます。

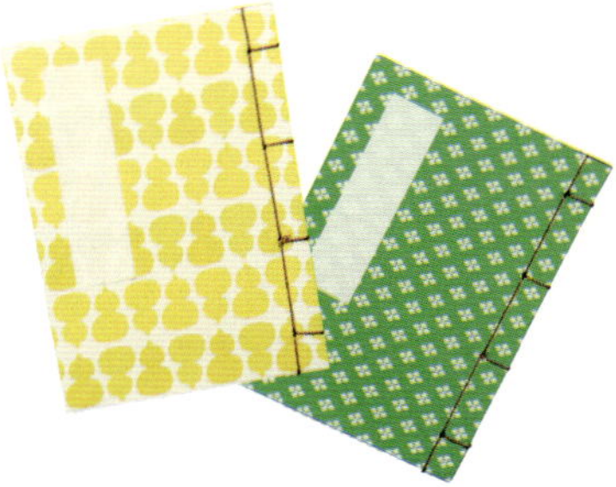

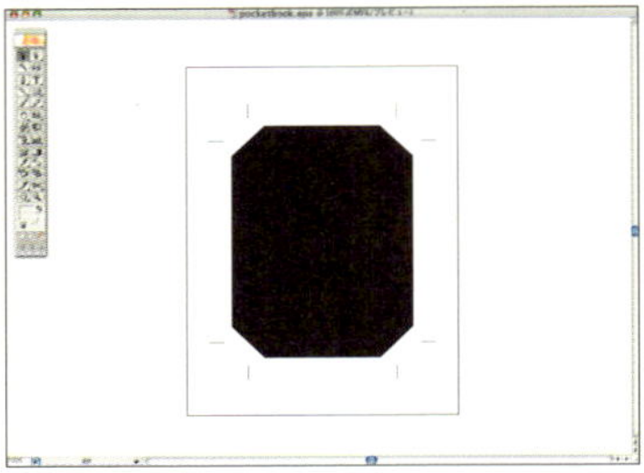

1

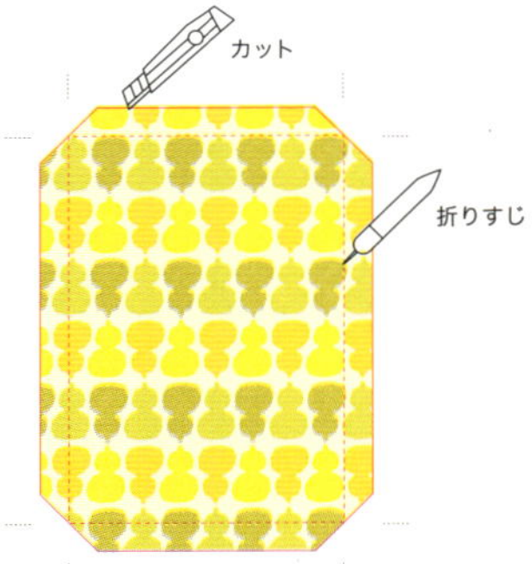

2

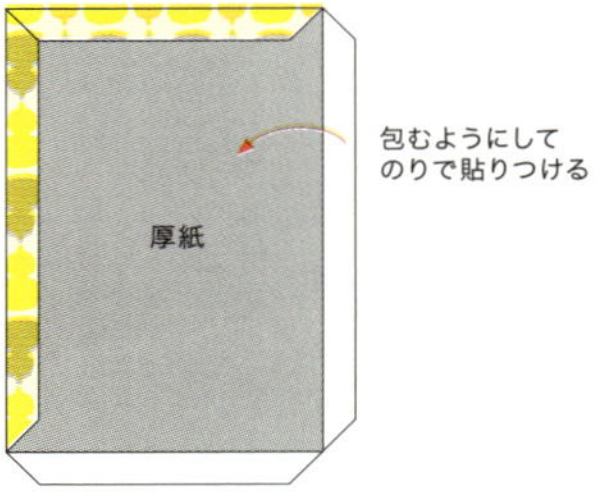

3

○用意するもの

インクジェット用和紙（表紙・裏表紙）、厚紙（128mm×91mmを2枚）、本文用紙（半紙などを30枚程度）、色和紙（角切れ）、製本針（ふとん針などでも可）、綴じ糸（たこ糸などの太めの糸）、カッター、はさみ、千枚通し（キリなどでも可）、のり、クリップ、定規、鉄筆（なければインクの切れたボールペンや芯を出さないシャープペンシルなどでも可）

1. 表紙・裏表紙に使う台紙データを開く

付属CD-ROMの「Template」フォルダの中にある「pocketbook.eps」をデスクトップにコピーし、Illustratorで開きます。

次に、使いたいパターンを「スウォッチ」に登録します（P.161参照）。

2. パターンで塗ってプリントする

選択ツールを選び、ドキュメント上のオブジェクトを選択します。選択したオブジェクトの塗りに、先ほど登録したパターンを設定します。これでデータの出来上がりです。プリンタにインクジェット用和紙をセットして、2枚プリントします。プリント後、それぞれ折りトンボに合わせて鉄筆で折りすじを入れて、境界線でカットします。

3. 表紙・裏表紙を作る

厚紙を2でプリントした表紙・裏表紙の折り線に合わせて、それぞれ包むようにしてのりで貼りつけます。

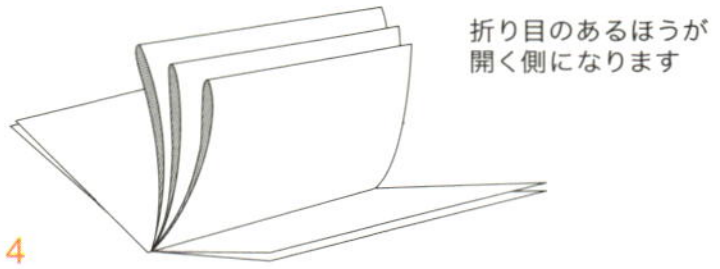

4

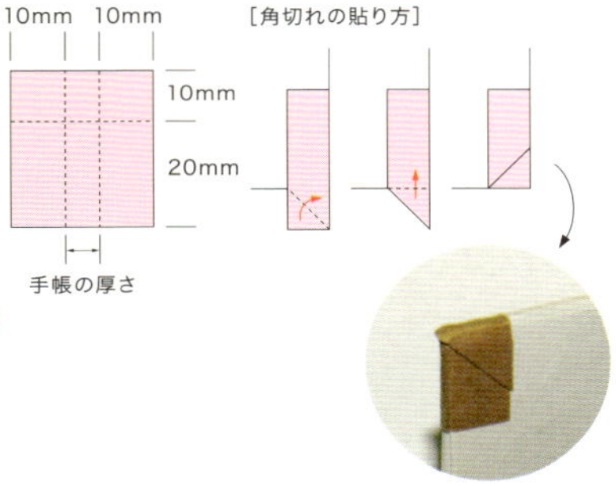

5

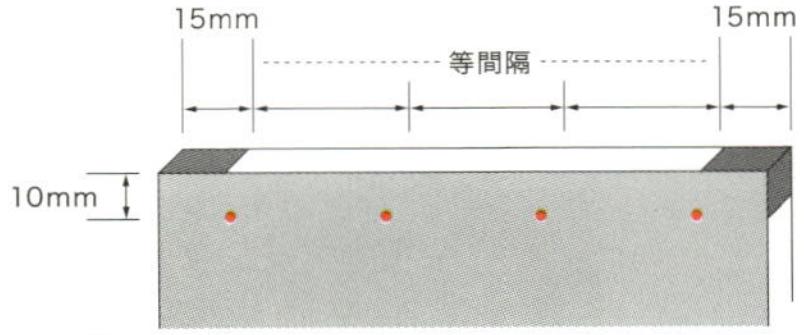

6

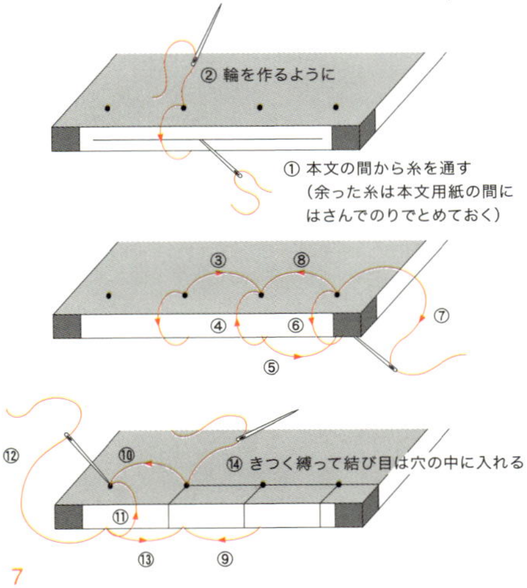

7

4. 本文用紙を作る

本文用紙を表紙と同じ大きさ(128mm×91mm)になるように2つ折りにします(30枚程度)。それらを束ね、クリップで固定します。和綴じでは、袋綴じのように本文を折った折り目のあるほうが開く側になります。

5. 角切れを貼る

和綴じでは、角を保護するために本文用紙に角切れを貼ります。角切れは装飾の役目も兼ねるので、表紙に合わせて色を選ぶなど工夫しましょう。

図のように色和紙で角切れを作り、4で作った本文用紙の綴じる側の上下にのりで貼っておきます。

6. 綴じ穴を開ける

表紙と本文用紙を重ねてクリップで動かないように固定します。上下15mm、右から10mmのところに千枚通しで綴じ穴を開けます。その間にも等間隔になるように2つ穴を開けておきます。

7. 本文と表紙を綴じる

左図のように、ひと筆書きのような要領で糸を通していきます。時折、糸を締めながら進めるときれいに仕上がります。

出来上がり!

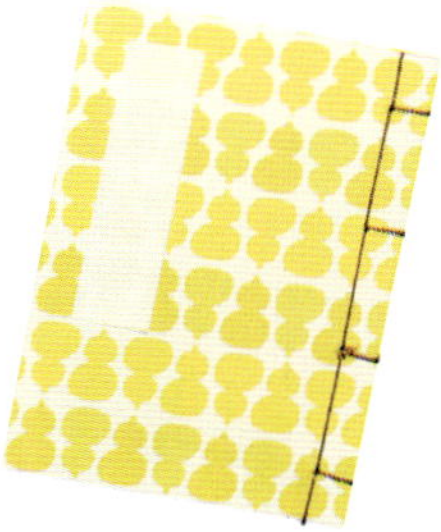

和・きもの柄
Japanese style

おしゃれなパターン素材集
Petit Pattern Book

001
jpn-style001

002
jpn-style002

003
jpn-style003

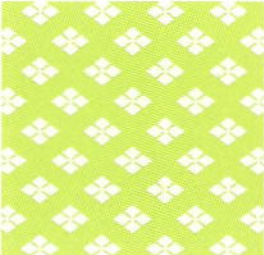
004
jpn-style004

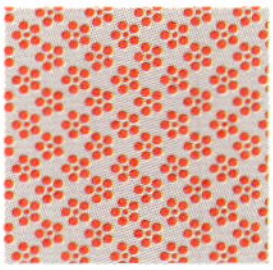
005
jpn-style005

006
jpn-style006

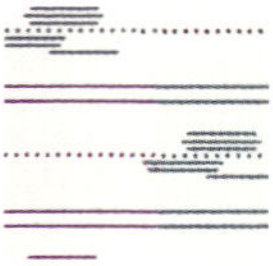
007
jpn-style007

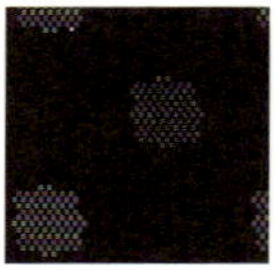
008
jpn-style008

009
jpn-style009

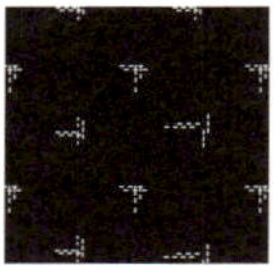
010
jpn-style010

011
jpn-style011

012
jpn-style012

013
jpn-style013

014
jpn-style014

015
jpn-style015

016
jpn-style016

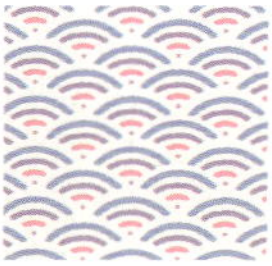
017
jpn-style017

018
jpn-style018

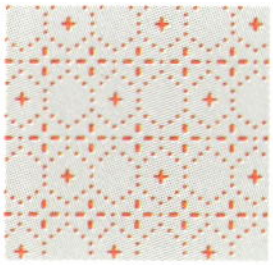
019
jpn-style019

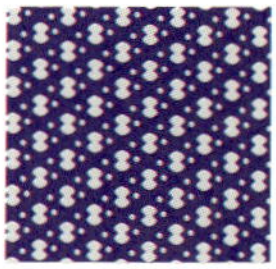
020
jpn-style020

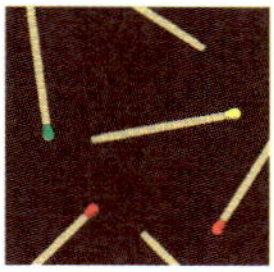

021
jpn-style021

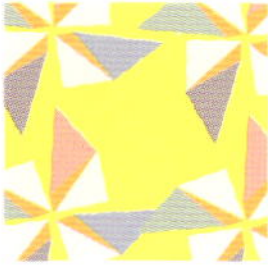

022
jpn-style022

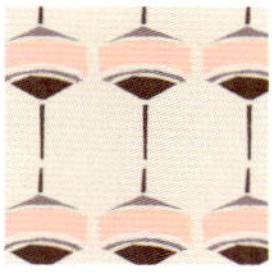

023
jpn-style023

024
jpn-style024

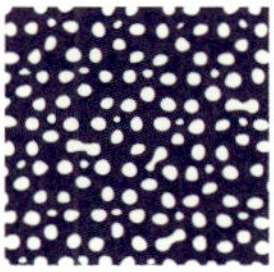

025
jpn-style025

026
jpn-style026

027
jpn-style027

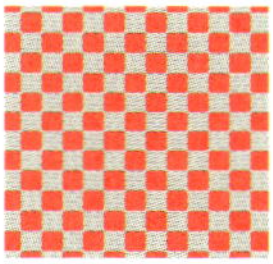

028
jpn-style028

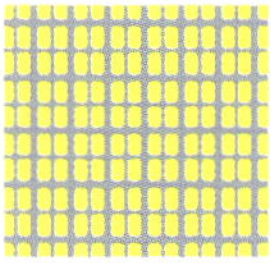

029
jpn-style029

030
jpn-style030

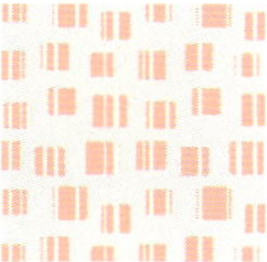

031
jpn-style031

032
jpn-style032

033
jpn-style033

034
jpn-style034

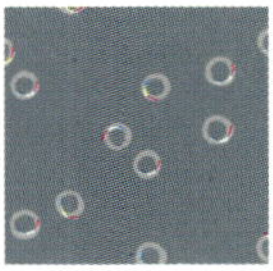

035
jpn-style035

036
jpn-style036

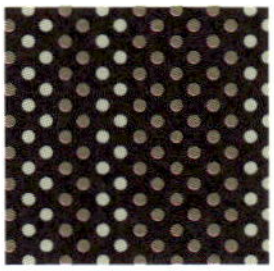

037
jpn-style037

038
jpn-style038

039
jpn-style039

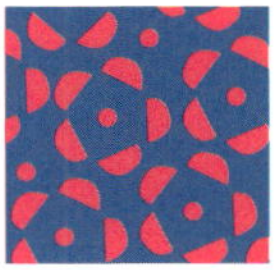

040
jpn-style040

041
jpn-style041

042
jpn-style042

043
jpn-style043

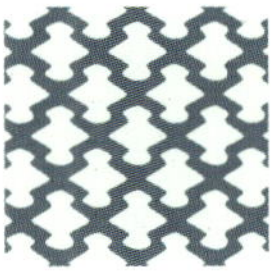

044
jpn-style044

045
jpn-style045

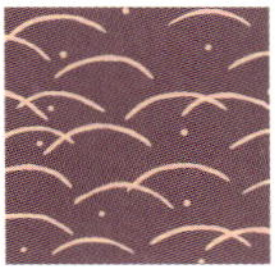

046
jpn-style046

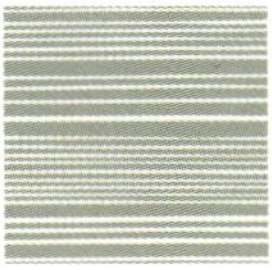

047
jpn-style047

048
jpn-style048

049
jpn-style049

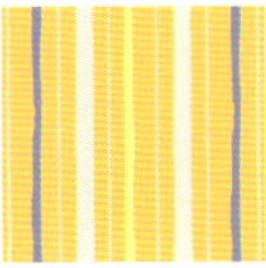

050
jpn-style050

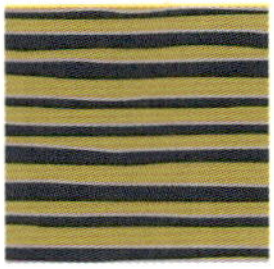
051
jpn-style051

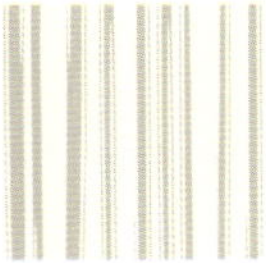
052
jpn-style052

053
jpn-style053

054
jpn-style054

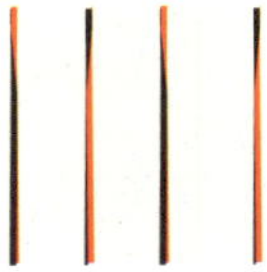
055
jpn-style055

056
jpn-style056

057
jpn-style057

058
jpn-style058

059
jpn-style059

060
jpn-style060

061
jpn-style061

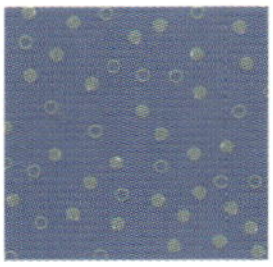
062
jpn-style062

063
jpn-style063

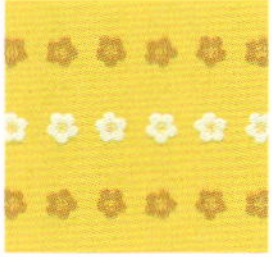
064
jpn-style064

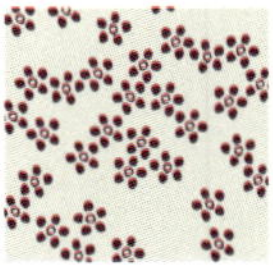
065
jpn-style065

066
jpn-style066

067
jpn-style067

068
jpn-style068

069
jpn-style069

070
jpn-style070

071
jpn-style071

072
jpn-style072

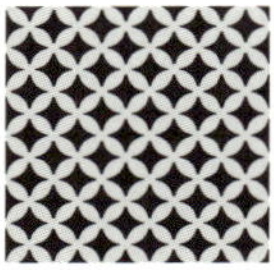
073
jpn-style073

074
jpn-style074

075
jpn-style075

076
jpn-style076

077
jpn-style077

078
jpn-style078

079
jpn-style079

080
jpn-style080

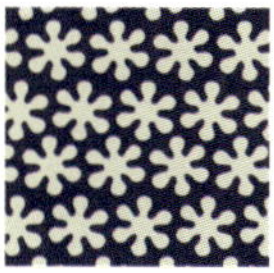
081
jpn-style081

082
jpn-style082

083
jpn-style083

084
jpn-style084

085
jpn-style085

086
jpn-style086

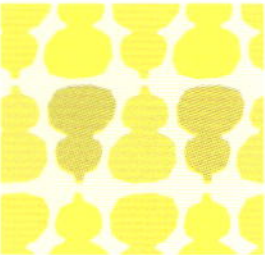
087
jpn-style087

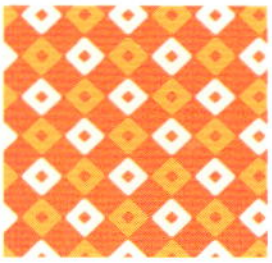
088
jpn-style088

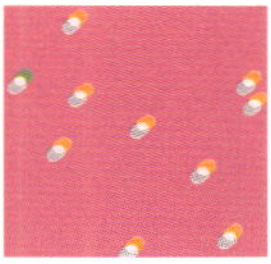
089
jpn-style089

090
jpn-style090

091
jpn-style091

092
jpn-style092

093
jpn-style093

094
jpn-style094

095
jpn-style095

096
jpn-style096

097
jpn-style097

098
jpn-style098

099
jpn-style099

100
jpn-style100

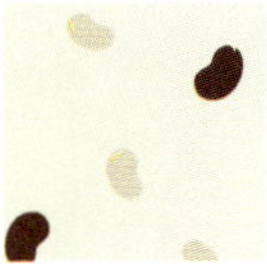
101
jpn-style101

102
jpn-style102

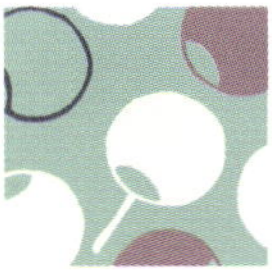
103
jpn-style103

104
jpn-style104

105
jpn-style105

106
jpn-style106

107
jpn-style107

108
jpn-style108

109
jpn-style109

110
jpn-style110

111
jpn-style111

112
jpn-style112

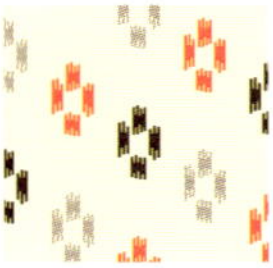
113
jpn-style113

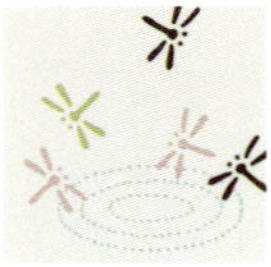
114
jpn-style114

115
jpn-style115

116
jpn-style116

117
jpn-style117

118
jpn-style118

119
jpn-style119

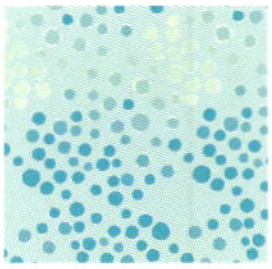
120
jpn-style120

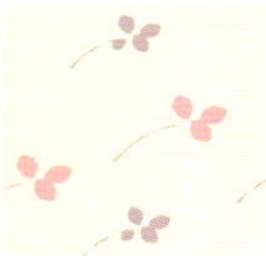
121
jpn-style121

122
jpn-style122

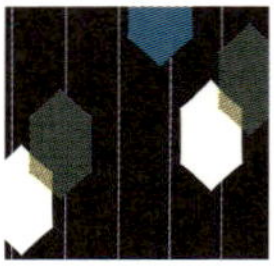
123
jpn-style123

124
jpn-style124

125
jpn-style125

126
jpn-style126

127
jpn-style127

128
jpn-style128

129
jpn-style129

130
jpn-style130

131
jpn-style131

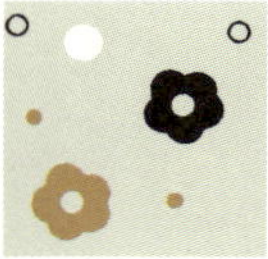
132
jpn-style132

133
jpn-style133

134
jpn-style134

135
jpn-style135

136
jpn-style136

137
jpn-style137

138
jpn-style138

139
jpn-style139

140
jpn-style140

『おしゃれなパターン素材集　和・きもの柄』
付属CD-ROM使用許諾書(ソフトウェアライセンス契約書)

1. ライセンス

1) 株式会社ビー・エヌ・エヌ新社(以下「弊社」という。)は、本製品を購入され、本使用許諾書記載の条件に合意されたお客様(以下「ユーザー」という。)に対し、本ソフトウェアを同時に1台のコンピュータ上でのみ使用できる、譲渡不能の非独占的権利を許諾します。

2) ユーザーは、2の「制限事由」に該当する場合を除き、本ソフトウェアに含まれる素材を加工・編集し、もしくは他の素材と組み合わせるなどして、主に以下のデザインに使用することができます。

○WEBなどのデジタルメディア

○店舗の内装、案内表示、レジにおける無料パッケージなどのグラフィックツール

○印刷物として頒布するチラシ、フライヤー、ポスター、DM、カタログ、パンフレットなどの広告・販売促進ツール

○個人制作・個人利用の雑貨、服、グリーティングカード、名刺など

(個人的・職業的・商業的用途の利用を認めますが、いずれも非売品のデザインに限ります。個人においても素材を利用した制作物の販売は行えません。次の制限事由をよくお読み下さい。)

2. 制限事由

以下の行為を禁止します。

1)本ソフトウェアを1台のコンピュータで使用するためのやむを得ぬ場合を除き、本ソフトウェアを複製すること

2)本使用許諾書に基づくライセンスを他に譲渡し、本製品の貸与もしくはその他の方法で本ソフトウェアを他者に使用させること

3)流通を目的とした商品のデザインに素材を利用すること(書籍や雑誌など、有料の印刷物を含む。)

4)商品パッケージおよび有料のギフトパッケージに素材を利用すること

5)素材をブランドイメージとして利用すること(可能性があると判断できるものも含む。)

6)素材を利用してポストカード、名刺、雑貨などの制作販売または制作サービスを行うこと

7)素材を利用してインターネットによるダウンロードサービスを行うこと(グリーティングカード・サービスを含む。)

8)素材をホームページ上で公開する場合に、オリジナルデータがダウンロード可能となる環境を作ること

9)ソフトウェア製品等を製造・販売するために素材を流用すること

10)素材そのものや素材を用いた制作物について意匠権などの権利を取得すること

11)素材を公序良俗に反する目的、誹謗・中傷目的で利用すること

※本素材を使用した商業デザインや商品販売等をお考えの際にはご相談に応じます。
事前に下記までご連絡ください。
○株式会社ビー・エヌ・エヌ新社(fax:03-5543-3108　e-mail:info@bnn.co.jp)

3. 著作権、その他の知的財産権

本ソフトウェアおよび素材に関する著作権、その他の知的財産権は、弊社または弊社への供給者の排他的財産として留保されています。素材を利用した制作物においてユーザーの著作権を明示する場合は、併せてパターンの著作権「©2006 MASTERPIECE INC.+Ac2」を明示してください。

4. 責任の制限

弊社および弊社への供給者は、請求原因の如何を問わず、本ソフトウェアの使用または使用の不能および素材の利用から生じるすべての損害や不利益(利益の逸失およびデータの損壊を含む。)につき、一切責任を負わないものとします。

5. 使用許諾の終了

ユーザーが本使用許諾書に違反した場合、弊社は、本使用許諾書に基づくユーザーのライセンスを終了させることができます。

Petit Pattern Book

How to use patterns

（Photoshop & Illustrator）

Before you start

○ Notes

- Please read the License Agreement on page 190 before you start.
- The explanation in this book is based on Mac OS X (10.4.5), Adobe Photoshop CS2, and Adobe Illustrator CS2. The functionality has also been verified with Windows XP Professional SP1. If your system is different, or if you have a question concerning the operation of the software, refer to the manuals corresponding to your OS and software.
- In the chapter "Let's use the patterns to make an original article" (p184-189), you will be using Illustrator and your printer.

○ Preparation

At first, set the attached CD-ROM and open "Japanese-style" folder. Pick up the patterns you need and copy them to your desktop.

Open the folder "Japanese-style" and you will find three folders: "JPEG", "EPS", and "Template". You are going to use the data inside "Template" from p184 as sample data later on.

Mac

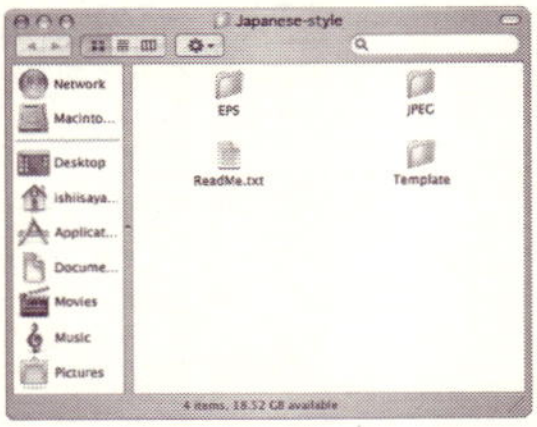

○ Different kinds of data

All the patterns in the book are prepared in the following two formats:
(EPS files are saved with Illustrator 8.0.)

JPEG

※In the JPEG file, you will find bitmap images which are printed on the surface of around 148× 210mm at 350 dpi (the resolution suitable for commercial printing). You can edit them with Adobe Photoshop and other bitmap software, and you can use it with many other types of software.

EPS

※In the EPS file, you will find vector images, which do not deteriorate when you increase or reduce the size. Open the file with Adobe Illustrator or other drawing software, and you will be able to customize the images freely (When you open the file with bitmap software such as Adobe Photoshop, the image will be developed as a bitmap image after the process called rasterizing).

Tiling with a pattern

All the files are repeated patterns which can be tiled. Register patterns in Photoshop, Illustrator or other graphic software, and you can tile one of the repeated patterns in the blink of an eye.

For those people who have never tiled with patterns, we shall explain how to do it using Photoshop and Illustrator, focusing on the settings.

● Open the data

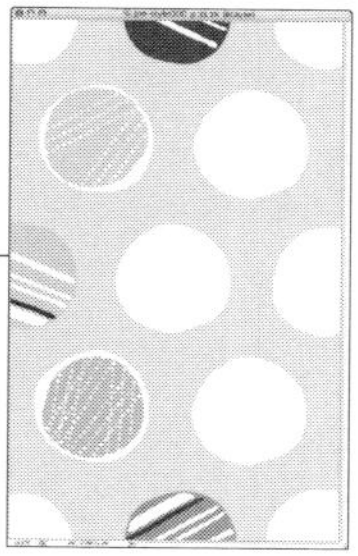

Photoshop

Select "Open" from the "File" menu, and open the pattern file (JPEG file here).

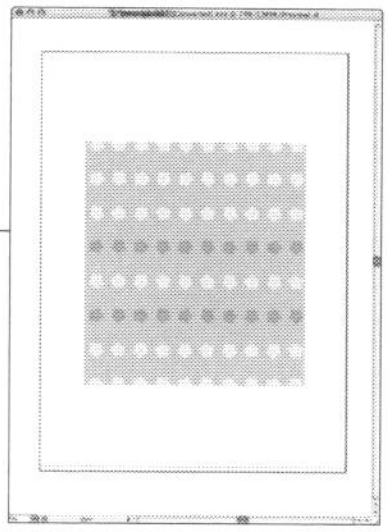

Illustrator

Select "Open" from the "File" menu, and open the pattern file (EPS file here). The pattern chosen will appear in the centre of the screen.

How to tile with
Photoshop

1. Save the pattern

Open your favorite pattern with Photoshop. Select the whole image by choosing "Select" → "All", and select "Edit" → "Define Pattern". Give the pattern an easily recognized name so that you can use it whenever you want.

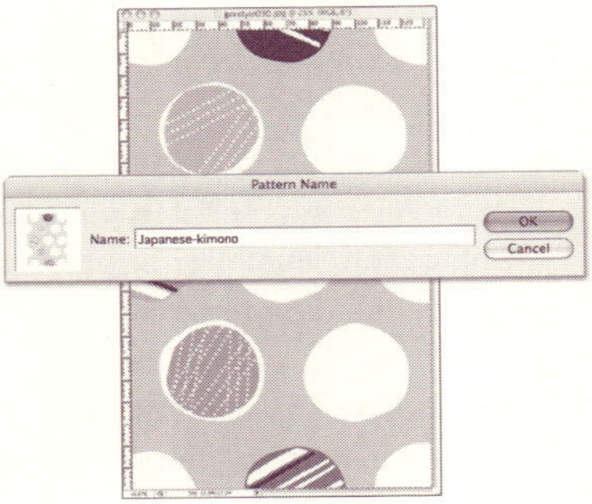

2. Select the saved pattern

Select "File" → "New" and create a blank image file to be filled with the pattern. Double click on Paint Bucket Tool and select "Pattern" from the options, and you are able to choose the pattern you have already defined.

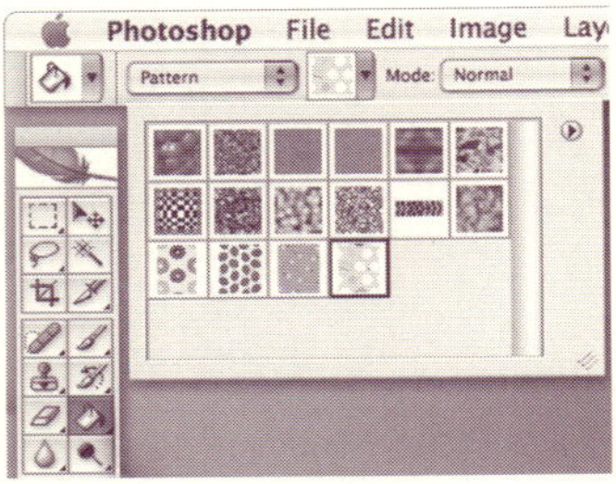

3. Tiling with the pattern

Click on the image with the Paint Bucket Tool and tile the whole image with the pattern.

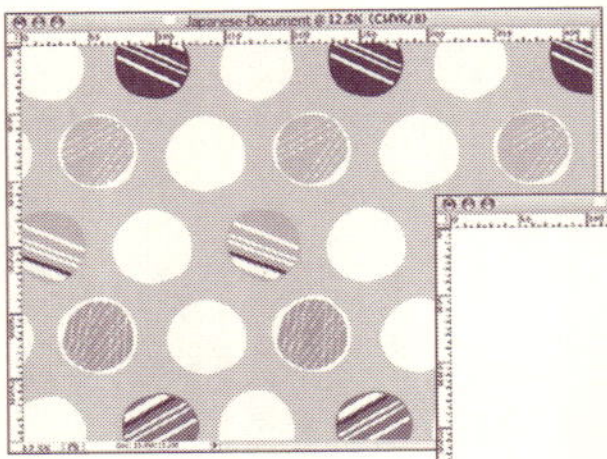
Figure 1

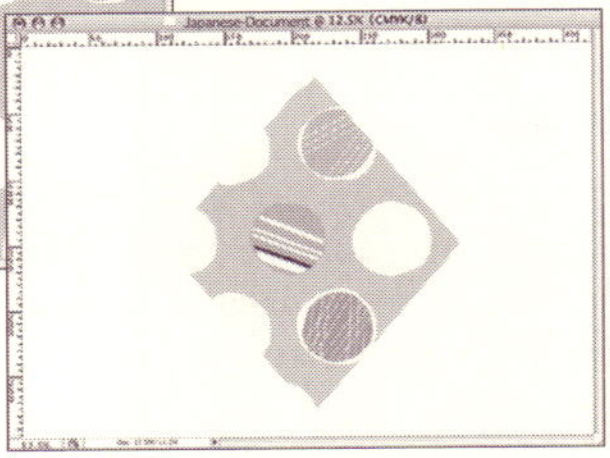
Figure 2

※Figure1 shows a blank 420×297mm file tiled with a pattern. If you use Select tools to select the part of the image to be tiled, you can tile only the part and the shape you have selected.

How to tile with

Illustrator

1. Save the pattern

Open your favorite pattern with Illustrator. Select the whole image by choosing “Select”→“All”, and “Edit”→“Copy” to copy the pattern.

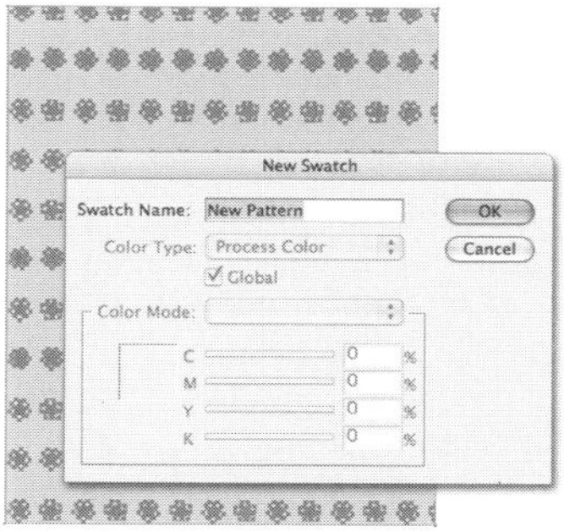

Create a blank document by selecting “File”→ “New”, and paste the pattern by selecting “Edit” → “Paste”. While the whole pattern is still selected, select “Edit”→“Define Pattern” to create a new swatch and give it an easily recognized name so that you can use it whenever you want.

2. Select the saved pattern

When you have saved the image, delete the pattern you pasted previously, as you do not need it any more. While the whole pattern is still selected, select “Edit”→ “Clear” and the pattern will be deleted.

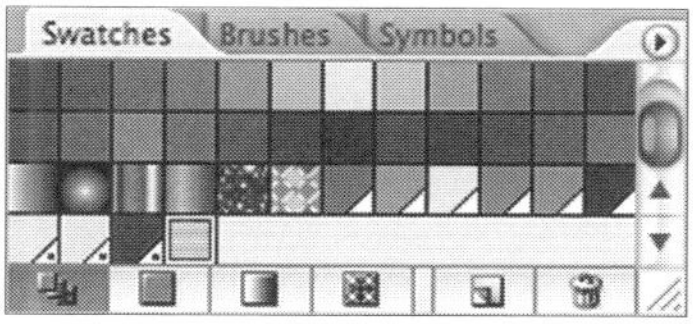

Select “Window”→“Swatches” to show the swatch pallet. Click the newly registered pattern on the swatch pallet.

3. Tiling with the pattern

Make an object to be tiled with the pattern.

Figure 1

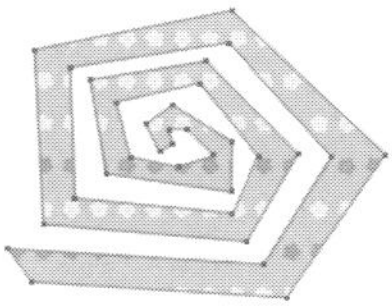

Figure 2

※Figure 1 shows a rectangular shape drawn with the Rectangular Tool. You can also draw a complicated object tiled with the pattern with other tools, as shown in Figure 2.

Extra 1

How to change the color of a pattern with Illustrator

Step 1

Open the EPS file with Illustrator (see p179). Select "Window"→"Swatches" to show the swatch pallet. Double click the swatch of the color you would like to change to show "Swatch Options".

※Most of the EPS files have different layers for each color and shape: you can arrange the patterns by changing the layer orders or hiding a layer.

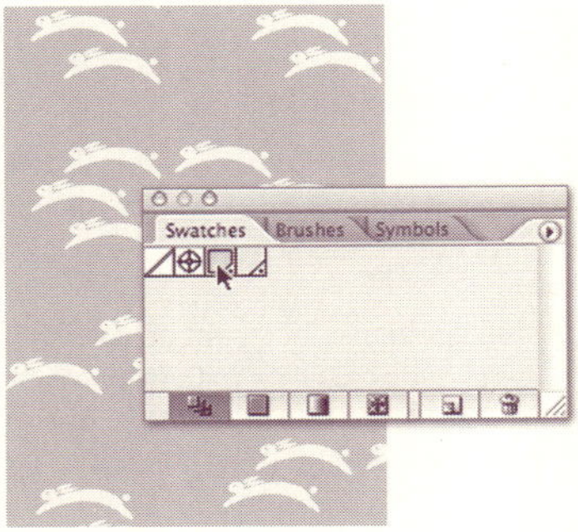

Step 2

Modify CMYK on the color pallet on "Swatch Options" to create your own color. You can select the "Preview" option beforehand to show the new color immediately. When you have obtained the color you want, click "OK".

※If you have opened the EPS file with Illustrator, you can modify the pattern any way you like: by changing the size, the shape, adding or taking out an element, etc. On the other hand, if you would like to save the modified pattern in Swatch for future use, avoid breaking the square artwork of its four sides, which would be juxtaposed on the tiling image.

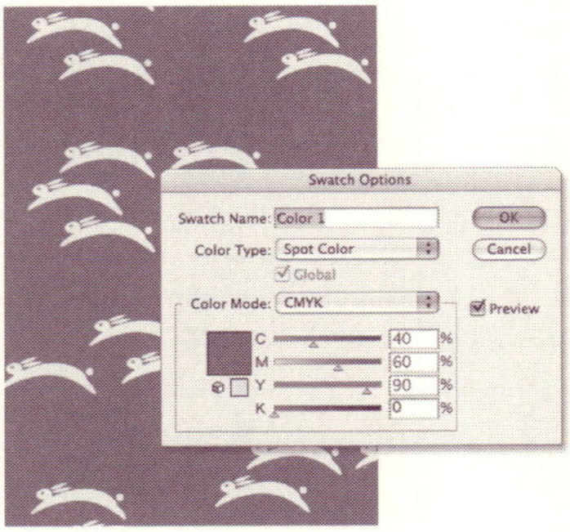

Step 3

Repeat 1-2 and create your own original pattern. Save it under a different name.

※While it is also possible to change the color of the JPEG file with Photoshop using the Paint Bucket Tool, the new color may be fuzzy in some patterns drawn using complicated lines. If this happens, select "Image" →"Adjustments"→"Color Balance" or "Hue/Saturation" to correct the color. Alternatively, open the EPS file of the same pattern with Illustrator, change the color, save as a JPEG file under a different name, and open and use it with Photoshop.

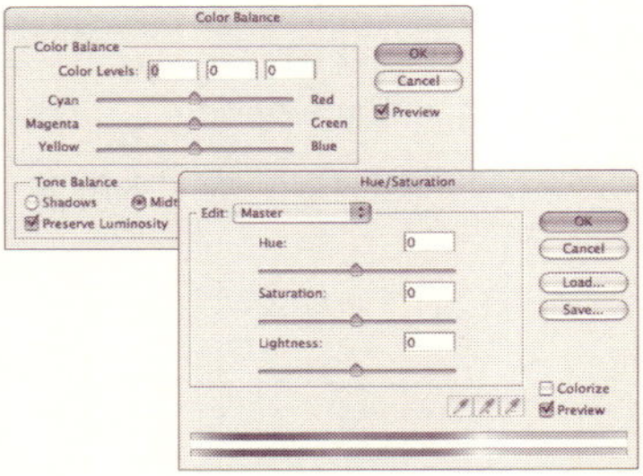

Extra 2

How to use the pattern as a desktop background of your computer

Step 1

Open the JPEG file with Photoshop (see p179), select "Image" → "Image Size". Change the resolution to "72 dpi", the resolution suitable for the monitor, and save it under a new name.

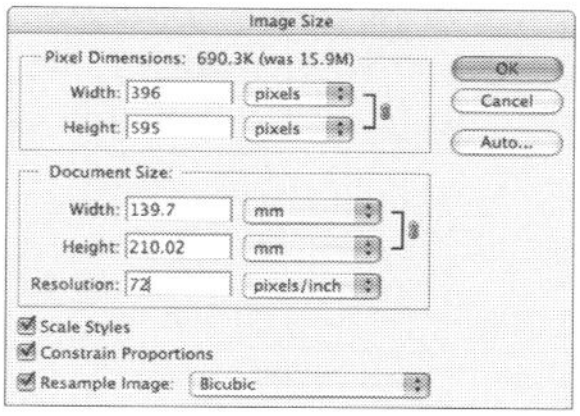

Step 2

-for Mac-

Go to the "Apple" menu and select "System Preferences"→"Desktop & Screen Saver". Select the saved file in Step1 for the desktop background, and choose "Tile" to make the pattern appear on the desktop.

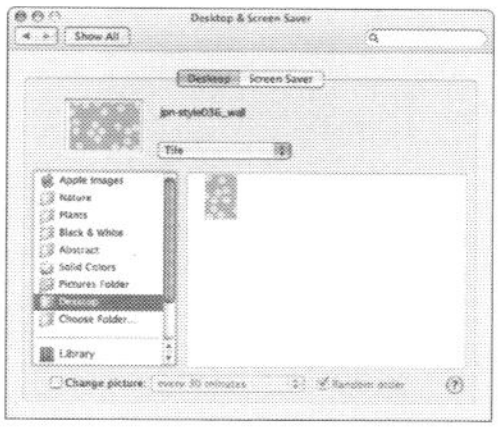

-for Windows-

Go to "Control Panel", and open "Display Properties" (you can also select it by right-clicking your mouse on the desktop). Click the "Desktop" tab, select the saved file in Step1 for the background, and chose "Tile" to show the pattern on the desktop.

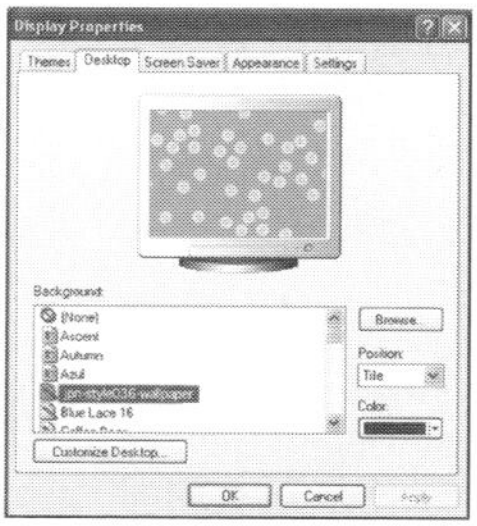

And More!

Using the pattern for the background of your website

The data at resolution "72 dpi" at Step 1 above can also be used as the background of a website.
In this case, it is recommended that you transfer the date to the GIF format, which is suitable for saving artworks other than photos.

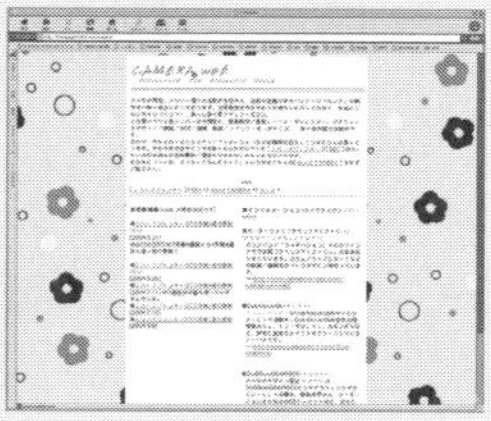

How to make a "pochi-bukuro" (small gift envelope)

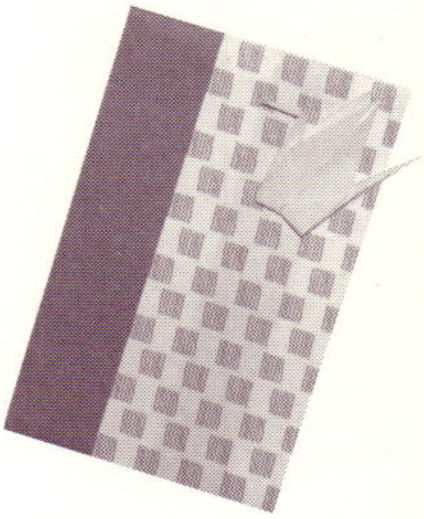

Put your small gift into this lovely little hand-made envelope as a present for a celebration, or a small thank-you to a friend. Select the pattern which you think best suits the person to whom you are giving the gift, so that it expresses your feelings properly.

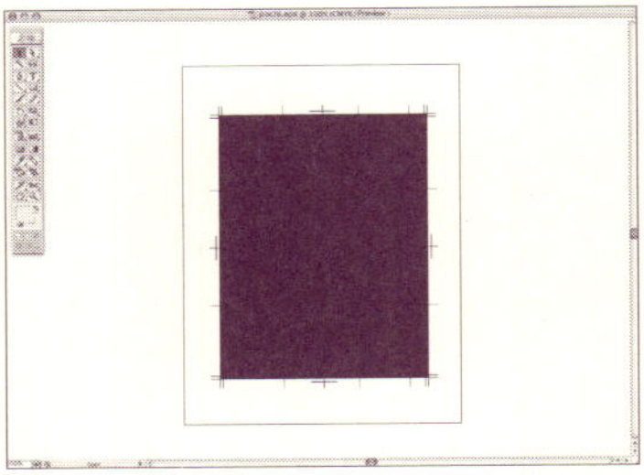

1

○You will need:

Printing paper (you can use ordinary paper, but if you use Japanese paper for Inkjet printers, you can expect more delicate look), a cutter, glue, and a tracer (You can also use a ballpoint pen that has run out of ink or a propelling pencil with no lead).

1. Open the mount data

Find the "pochi.eps" file in the "Template" folder in the attached CD-ROM. Copy it on to the hard disk, and open it with Illustrator.

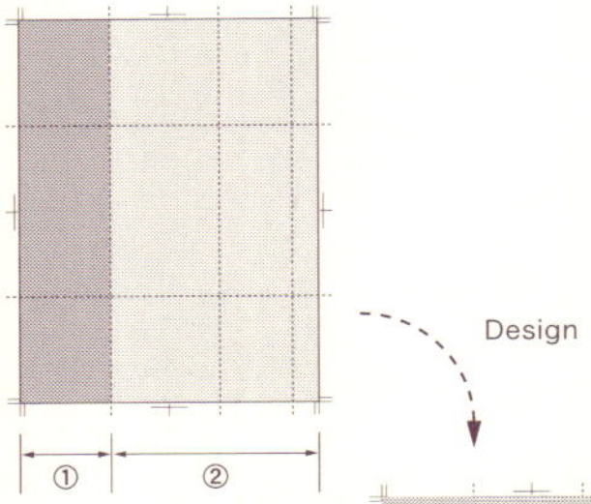

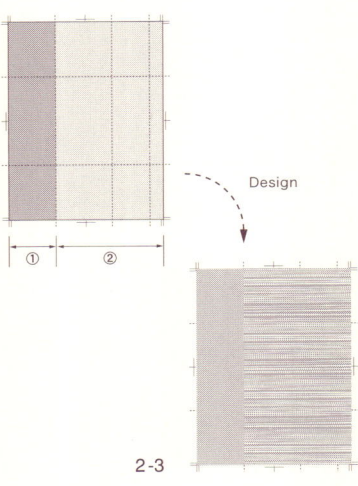

2-3

2. Design with patterns

Register the pattern you have chosen in "Swatch" (see p181).

The mount in the CD-ROM is already marked with trimming lines, which serve as a guideline for creasing and cutting.

In the mount, you'll find two objects (①&②). To paint these objects, select the pattern which you have saved, and the color. At the end of the process, the two objects are to be overlapped. Feel free to create the design that pleases you most.

4
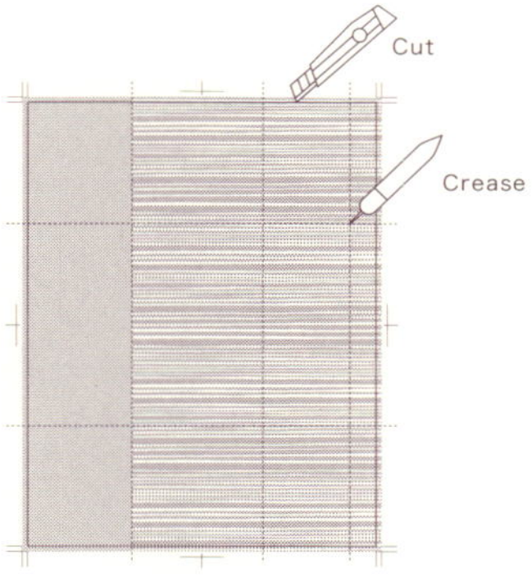

5
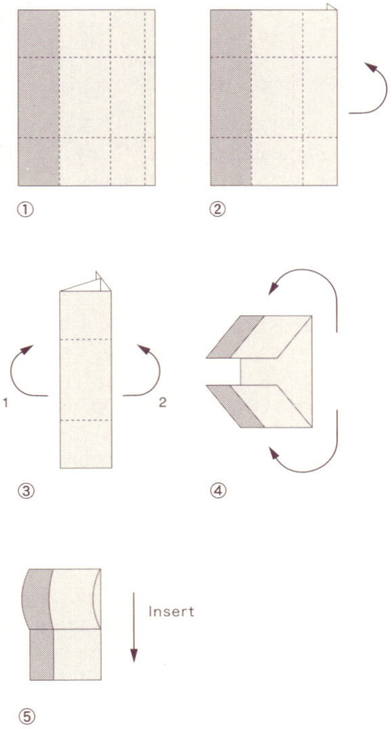

3.Print

Print the finished design on paper. Here we're using Japanese paper for Inkjet printers.

4. Crease and cut

The mount in the CD-ROM is already marked with trimming lines, which serve as guidelines for creasing and cutting. Place the ruler along the dotted trimming lines so that you can crease the paper with a tracer. Fold it to make a package. This process makes easier to fold the paper to finish the envelope afterwards.

Cut carefully placing the ruler just inside the trimming lines.

5. Fold along the creases

Fold along the creases as shown in the figures on the left.

Now you are ready to put something inside your little envelope!

Use different combinations of the patterns for different styles. Try decorating the envelope with ribbon or with a small folded origami to make it look even more charming.

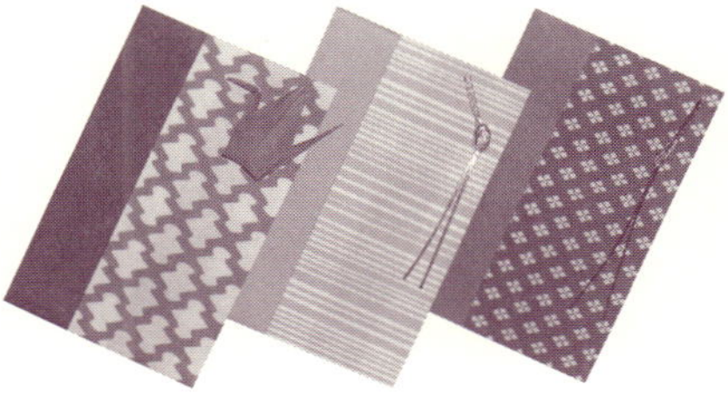

How to make a "scented sachet"

Slip this Japanese-style sachet under the pillow or in your handbag to enjoy its sweet fragrance. Choose a heart-warming color so that you feel relaxed whenever you look at it.

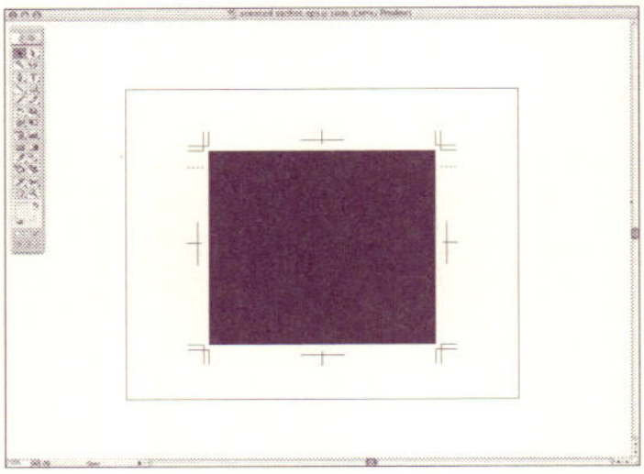

1

◯You will need:

Canvas cloth for use with a printer, string, a piece of tailor's chalk, a sewing machine, glue for the cloth, a pair of scissors and a cutter

1. Open the mount data

Find the "sachet.eps" file in the "Template" folder in the attached CD-ROM. Copy it on to the hard disk, and open it with Illustrator.

2

2. Tile with the pattern

Register the pattern you like in "Swatch" (see p181).

Click on the Select tool and select the object on the document. Select the pattern which you have saved to paint the selected object.

3

3. Printing on canvas

Set the cloth in the printer and print the design out. We are using canvas with a covering of PET film on the back. Watch out: all cloth for printing has a printing side (Stick to the detailed settings in the manual for the product you are using).

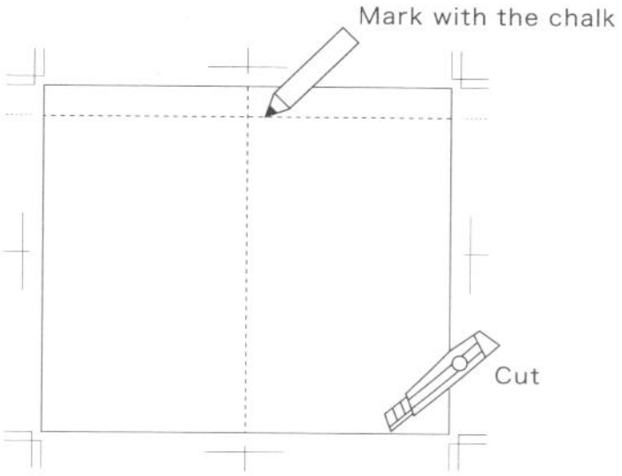

4

4. Cutting

The mount in the CD-ROM is already marked with trimming lines, which serve as guidelines for creasing and cutting. Firstly, mark out lines according to the trimming lines, so that you can make creases with the chalk.

Secondly, placing the ruler inside the corner trimming lines, then cut off the blank parts of the paper.

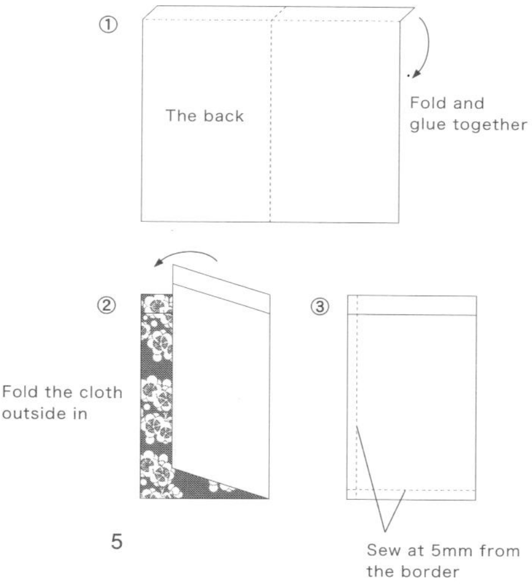

5

5. Sewing

After peel off the PET film on the back, serving the chalked line as a guideline, fold and sew the cloth as shown in the figures ①-③. Then turn the cloth inside out.

6. Filling and tying the sachet

Once the sachet is ready, fill it with something that smells nice. Break up incense sticks and put them inside. That is a popular use, but you could also try incense corns or potpourri.

Finally, tie the sachet with the string.

6

Now the scented sachet is ready!

Try putting it in your pocket to enjoy the fragrance in secret. It will also work well if you hang it inside a wardrobe.

How to make a "pocket book"

Use this as a notebook or a personal diary.
Make a note of anything you want in this pocket book, which is bound in Japanese style and will help to relax you. Put it on your desk to cheer you up.

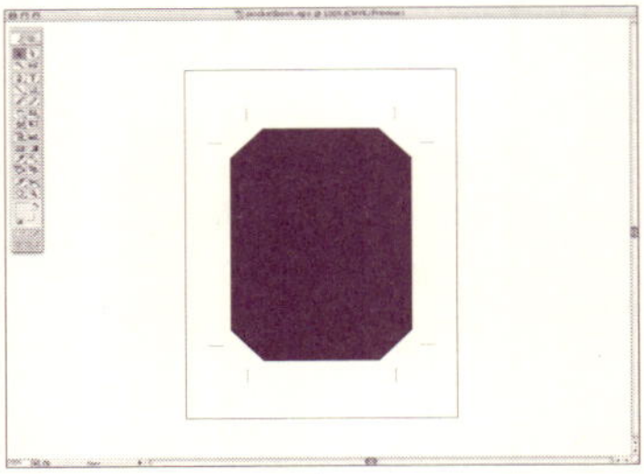

1

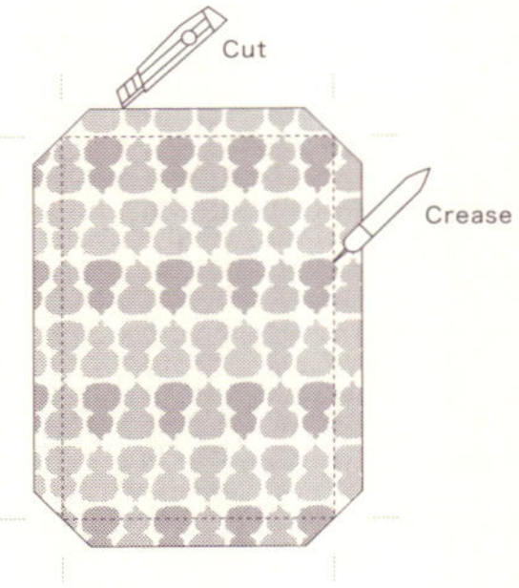

2

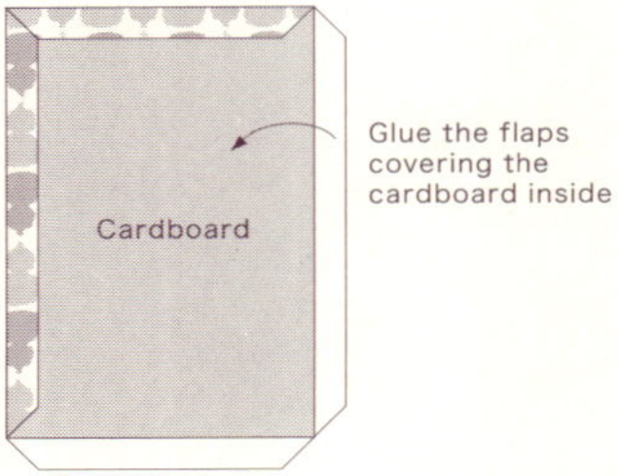

3

○You will need:

Japanese paper for Inkjet printers (for the covers), two sheets of cardboard (128mm× 91mm), paper for the pages (about 30sheets of standard-size Japanese writing paper), colored Japanese paper (to protect the edges), a book binding needle (a heavy darning needle will do), thread for binding (heavy cobbler's thread, etc.), a cutter, a pair of scissors, a bodkin (or an awl), glue, paper clips, a ruler and a tracer (you can also use a ballpoint pen that has run out of ink or a propelling pencil with no lead).

1. Open the mount data

Find the "pocketbook.eps" file in the "Template" folder in the attached CD-ROM. Copy it on to the hard disk, and open it with Illustrator.

Register the pattern you like in "Swatch" (see p181).

2. Tile with the pattern and print

Click on the Select tool and select the object on the document. Select the pattern which you have saved to paint the selected object. The data is now ready to be printed. Print it on the two sheets of Japanese paper for Inkjet printers. Crease with a tracer along the trimming lines and cut out.

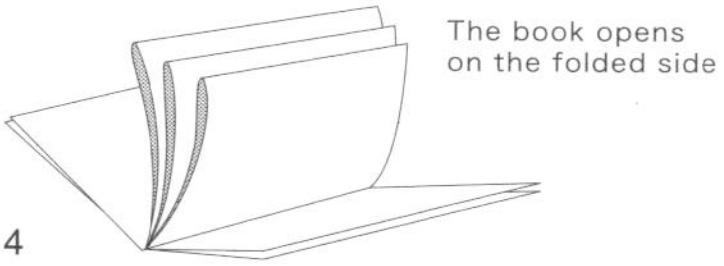

4

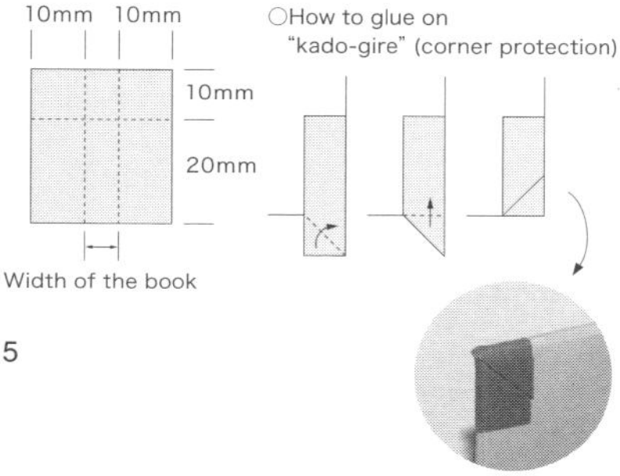

5

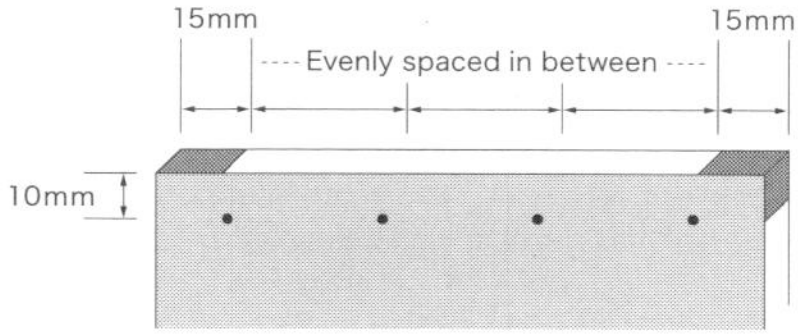

6

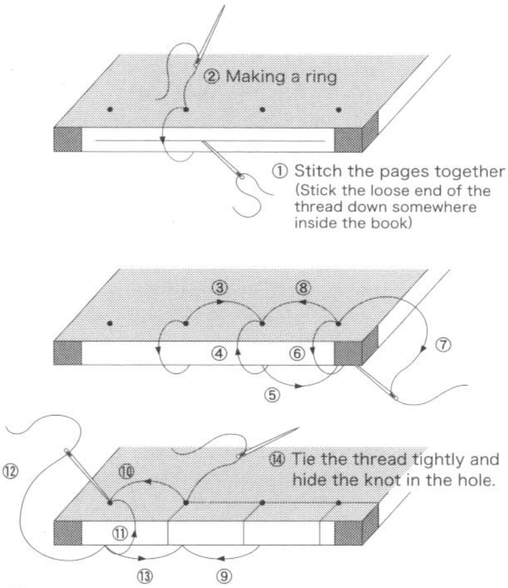

7

3. Make the covers

Place a sheet of cardboard on each printed sheet, along the creases, and glue the flaps covering the cardboard inside.

4. Make the pages

Fold the paper (about 30 sheets) in two, to make them the same size as the covers. Stack the book and pages together and pin it all together with the paper clips. In Japanese style, the book opens on the folded side like a bound-pocket book.

5. Glue on the edge protection

In Japanese book binding, the edges of the page are protected by small pieces of paper called "kado-gire" which are also decorative. Choose the paper that best goes with the covers.

Make "kado-gire" with Japanese paper as shown in the figures on the left and glue them on the top and the bottom edges of the pages, on the bound-side.

6. Punch holes

Stack the book together with the pages between the covers and hold it together with the paper clips. Punch two holes both at 10mm from the border on the right and each at 15mm from the border on the top and bottom. Punch two more holes at even distances in between.

7. Bind the book

Bind the book stitching around the spine as shown on the left. Pull the thread from time to time for perfect results.

Now the book is ready for your pocket!

Petit Pattern Book: Japanese Style
License Agreement of the Software

1. License

1) This License Agreement is a legal agreement between you (the "User"), who purchased the product Petit Pattern Book: Japanese Style, and BNN, Inc. ("BNN"), in respect of the attached CD-ROM entitled Petit Pattern Book: Japanese Style ("Software"). The User agrees to be bound by the terms of this License Agreement by installing, copying, or using the Software. BNN grants the User the right to use a copy of the Software on one personal computer for the exclusive use of the User.

2) The User may modify, edit, or combine the materials included in the Software except the cases specified in "2. Limitations" ; the User has the right to use the Software principally for design of the following objects.
  ○ Digital media including websites.
  ○ Use them as a graphic tool for creating shop interiors, signs, or for free wrapping services at the counter
  ○ Leaflets, flyers, posters, direct mail, catalogues, pamphlets, and other tools for advertisement or sales promotion.
  ○ Goods, clothes, greeting cards, name cards and other articles for personal production and use. (The Software may be used for personal, professional, and commercial purposes, provided that the articles produced are not offered for sale. The User may not sell articles made with the Software, even when of a personal nature. Please read the following Limitations carefully.)

2. Limitations

The User is not licensed to do any of the following:
1) Copy the Software, unless copying it is unavoidable to enable it to be used on one personal computer.
2) License, or otherwise by any means permit, any other person to use the Software.
3) Use the Software to design of products for distribution. (for printed matter on sale, e.g. books and magazines)
4) For wrapping merchandise or paid gift-wrapping services
5) As a part of the brand image of a company (even when this is still under consideration for the future).
6) Use the Software for the commercial production of postcards, name cards, or any other articles, or sell any such articles made using the Software.
7) Provide downloading services using the Software (including greeting card services).
8) Create an environment which allows the original data to be downloaded when you show one of the Software patterns on a home page.
9) Use the Software in order to produce any software or other products for sale.
10) Acquire the copyright in any material in the Software or any object you have created using the Software.
11) Use the Software to create obscene, scandalous, abusive or slanderous works.

We will be more than happy to discuss your needs with you if you are interested in using our materials for commercial designs or product sales. Please contact us on the following fax number or e-mail.
○ BNN, Inc. (fax : 03-5543-3108 e-mail : info@bnn.co.jp)

3. Copyright and other intellectual property

BNN or its suppliers reserves the copyright and other intellectual property rights in the Software. When specifying the User's copyright of a product made using the Software, please also write "©2006 MASTERPIECE INC. + Ac2".

4. Exclusion of damages

In no event shall BNN be liable for any damages whatsoever (including but not limited to, damages for loss of profit or loss of data) related to the use or inability to use of the Software or use of materials in the Software.

5. Termination of this License Agreement

If the User breaches this License Agreement, BNN has the right to withdraw the User's License granted on the basis hereof.

おしゃれなパターン素材集
Petit Pattern Book

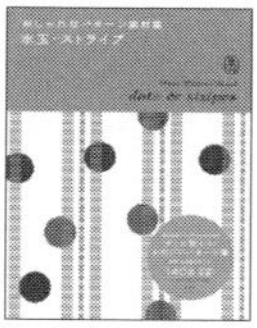

水玉・ストライプ
Dots & Stripes
ISBN：4-86100-384-9

花柄・リーフ
Flowers & Leaves
ISBN：978-4-86100-385-1

北欧・ファブリック
Scandinavian Style
ISBN：978-4-86100-386-8

キッズ・トイ
Kids & Toys
ISBN：978-4-86100-506-0

チェック・ニット
Check & Knit
ISBN：978-4-86100-507-7

シンプル・ナチュラル
Simple & Natural
ISBN：978-4-86100-522-0

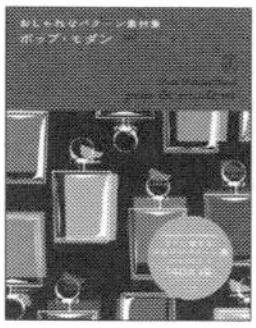

ポップ・モダン
Pop & Modern
ISBN：978-4-86100-523-7

おしゃれなパターン素材集
和・きもの柄

2006年9月25日　初版第1刷発行
2007年9月25日　初版第3刷発行

アートディレクション　中山正成（2m09cmGRAPHICS）

ブックデザイン　山際昇太（2m09cmGRAPHICS）

パターンデザイン　有限会社マスターピース ＋ 北岡武史（Ac2）

撮影アシスタント　金子りえ

翻訳　R.I.C.出版株式会社

発行人　籔内康一

発行所　株式会社ビー・エヌ・エヌ新社
〒104-0042
東京都中央区入船3-7-2　35山京ビル
fax 03-5543-3108　e-mail info@bnn.co.jp

印刷・製本　株式会社 シナノ

Printed in Japan
ISBN　978-4-86100-390-5